Selected Devotions

GARY HANKINS

ISBN 979-8-89345-324-9 (paperback)
ISBN 979-8-89345-325-6 (digital)

Copyright © 2024 by Gary Hankins

All rights reserved. No part of this publication may be reproduced, distributed, or transmitted in any form or by any means, including photocopying, recording, or other electronic or mechanical methods without the prior written permission of the publisher. For permission requests, solicit the publisher via the address below.

Christian Faith Publishing
832 Park Avenue
Meadville, PA 16335
www.christianfaithpublishing.com

Printed in the United States of America

I pray that the words here are our Father's, not mine.

Please attend the Christian church of your choosing so that you may hear the Word of God and walk along the way in faith, with Jesus Christ.

²⁵ Jesus said to her, "I am the resurrection and the life. He who believes in Me, though he may die, he shall live. ²⁶ And whoever lives and believes in Me shall never die. Do you believe this?" (John 11:25–26)

¹⁷ So then faith comes by hearing, and hearing by the word of God. (Romans 10:17)

⁸ For by grace you have been saved through faith, and that not of yourselves; it is the gift of God, ⁹ not of works, lest anyone should boast. (Ephesians 2:8–9)

⁶ Jesus said to him, "I am the way, the truth, and the life. No one comes to the Father except through Me." (John 14:6)

Around the Campfire

Many of us have experienced camping out in the woods where the day is full of sun, fun, and adventures. But as evening skies darken, we retreat to gather around the campfire built to provide us light, warmth, and perhaps nourishment cooked over the open fire. Now, the world around us is now less inviting, even threatening. Who wants to venture alone into the darkness beyond the light? Not me!

God's universe offers light from countless suns which shine against the infinite darkness, many of them have planets which gather around their light and warmth. Earth is blessed to be one of those planets which orbits at just the right distance from our "campfire" to be warmed and sustained by its light.

Yet scientists warn us that our sun won't last forever. They tell us of a time in the distant future when our sun will explode, turning our green earth into a cold cinder. But the light of Jesus Christ, God's only begotten Son, will never dim. He is with us always (Matthew 28:20).

Let His light and love warm you and keep you in this New Year for it will never die, nor will we who believe in Him and repent of our sins (John 11:26).

When we depart from this flesh, He will bring us home to Him and all who have gone before in Him, where time nor tears have any place. Where we will never again be separated from one another.

Happy new year in Jesus Christ, our risen Lord and Savior! You make every year happy too, as we share our love in Him forever.

Lamb of God

The Old Testament prescribes the blood sacrifices that God and how those sacrifices were to be made. Just as sin is endless, the sacrifices were also without end.

It was the blood of a sacrificial lamb that was spread on the doorposts of the Jews as Moses was delivering God's commandment to release His people to the Pharaoh of Egypt that had enslaved them. Moses warned the pharaoh that God's spirit would pass through Egypt and slay the firstborn of every man or beast if the pharaoh did not relent. The Jews painted their doorposts with the blood of a lamb. "Your lamb shall be without blemish, a male a year old" (Exodus 12:5). The homes with the blood of the sacrificial lambs applied as instructed were passed over in the night. Their firstborn were left unharmed.

Blood was the Old Testament's cure for the curse of sin. Sin and the blood necessary to seek forgiveness of sins committed were endless. The term "transactional relationship" coined by psychiatrists and sociologists is used today.

That was true until John the Baptist announced the holy nature of Jesus Christ's ministry to all mankind. "²⁹ The next day John saw Jesus coming toward him, and said, Behold! The Lamb of God who takes away the sin of the world!" (John 1:29). I don't believe those who heard these words of blessing could have comprehended their full meaning, as John did.

Many of us still struggle to understand and accept the true nature of Jesus Christ, our risen Lord and Savior. The Passover was a shadow cast by the holy light of Jesus Christ whose birth into our flesh was still thousands of years away. His light is present from the beginning of God's creation and shines throughout time without end. While the Passover lamb's shed blood protected a few in a single circumstance, the blood of Jesus Christ protects everyone who believes in Him forever.

> ¹⁵ That whosoever believeth in him should not perish, but have eternal life. ¹⁶ For God so loved the world, that he gave his only begotten Son, that whosoever believeth in him should not perish, but have everlasting life. ¹⁷ For God sent not his Son into the world to condemn the world; but that the world through him might be saved. (John 3:15–17)

Jesus took every sin upon Himself on the cross, from Eden until Christ returns to make His kingdom on earth in His final judgment. We who believe and repent in Him before he returns will live in His kingdom together forever. Those who do not, will not.

The warmth and peace of our Christmas just past is also just a shadow the light of Christ shining upon his here and now. At His second coming, we shall be bathed in His light forever.

Every day is Christmas. Each day, we may open His gift of grace again to feel His love. Let us thank Jesus together daily.

Every Promise Kept

"And I will put enmity between you and the woman, and between your offspring and hers; he will crush your head, and you will strike his heel." (Genesis 3:15)

[14] Therefore the Lord Himself will give you a sign: Behold, the virgin shall conceive and bear a Son, and shall call His name Immanuel. (Isaiah 7:14)

[30] The angel said to her, "Don't be afraid, Mary; God has shown you his grace. [31] Listen! You will become pregnant and give birth to a son, and you will name him Jesus. [32] He will be great and will be called the Son of the Most High. The Lord God will give him the throne of King David, his ancestor. [33] He will rule over the people of Jacob forever, and his kingdom will never end." [34] Mary said to the angel, "How will this happen since I am a virgin?" (Luke 1:30–34)

[47] Truly, truly I say to you, the one who believes in Me has everlasting life. (John 6:47)

[6] Jesus saith unto him, I am the way, the truth, and the life: no man cometh unto the Father, but by me. (John 14:6)

[18] Then Jesus came to them and said, "All authority in heaven and on earth has been given to me. [19] Therefore go and make disciples of all nations, baptizing them in the name of the Father and of the Son and of the Holy Spirit, [20] and teaching them to obey everything I have com-

manded you. And surely I am with you always, to the very end of the age." (Matthew 28:18–20)

Jesus is a gift from God. May we celebrate Christmas every day, forever and ever. Amen!

Seek Not Glory

I remember Sunday school was full of wonderful stories and colorful pictures of Jesus Christ performing miracles. Sunday after Sunday, we were treated to episodes of the Superhero above all superheroes.

Superman was cool and exciting as he battled supervillains. He wore a neat costume and flew faster than a speeding bullet. He was invulnerable (that's the first time I recall that word) and hid his superpowers as the unassuming Clark Kent.

Jesus healed the sick, raised the dead. He performed for our young minds in weekly installments and amazed us. And He is real! It all really happened!

Yet as I grew and allegedly matured, I put away the things of my childhood. Life separated me from Sunday school and circumstances focused me on more pressing personal matters than Bible stories. After all, none of those wondrous miracles saved me, even if they are true. No, it was not glory that mattered in the comic books or the Bible.

Those glorious miracles did focus attention on the message of Jesus Christ. The attention He attracted to the Truth He preached made powerful people nervous as He pointed out their glory did not make them right.

> A rich young man from a fine family approached Jesus, asking what he must do to have eternal life. Jesus told him he must obey every commandment and law. The young man claimed that he did that. Then, [21] Jesus told him, "If you want to be perfect, go and sell all your

possessions and give the money to the poor, and you will have treasure in heaven. Then come, follow me." ²² But when the young man heard this, he went away sad, for he had many possessions. (Matthew 19:21–22)

Later, ²⁴ Then Jesus told his disciples, "If anyone would come after me, let him deny himself and take up his cross and follow me. ²⁵ For whoever would save his life will lose it, but whoever loses his life for my sake will find it. ²⁶ For what will it profit a man if he gains the whole world and forfeits his soul? Or what shall a man give in return for his soul?" (Matthew 16:24–26)

It wasn't easy for Jesus. On the night in which He was betrayed, ³⁹ And he went a little farther, and fell on his face, and prayed, saying, O my Father, if it be possible, let this cup pass from me: nevertheless not as I will, but as thou wilt. (Matthew 26:39)

In this low moment, in the darkness, Jesus revealed how human He is and how devoted He is to His Father's will. The glory we inherit eternally is Jesus Christ's glory shining upon us to purify and preserve us in Him forever as His born-again brothers and sisters in God's own family.

Thank you, Jesus!

Adiaphora

"Adiaphora" is a word that I did not know until I read today's devotion from Lutheran Hour Ministries.

It is most certainly something that many of us find personally familiar once we know its definition. "Adiaphora" describes those things which are not clearly addressed in the Bible. This is not a new phenomenon.

The Apostle Paul wrote this to the congregations in Rome two thousand years ago:

> [14] Accept the one whose faith is weak, without quarreling over disputable matters. [2] One person's faith allows them to eat anything, but another, whose faith is weak, eats only vegetables. [3] The one who eats everything must not treat with contempt the one who does not, and the one who does not eat everything must not judge the one who does, for God has accepted them. [4] Who are you to judge someone else's servant? (Romans 14:1–4)

Adiaphora is present throughout our congregations. It resides in the pews and the church councils.

It is Jesus Christ who will judge us all when He returns to us. We have a personal relationship with God through Jesus. It is deeper and more honest than any human relationship.

Jesus taught us clearly and worked diligently to teach us what our Father in Heaven finds acceptable and what is not. He leaves us with clarity on those things which He finds sinful. It is called the Law.

> Jesus tell us, [17] Think not that I am come to destroy the law, or the prophets: I am not come to destroy, but to fulfil. [18] For verily I say unto you, Till heaven and earth pass, one jot or one tittle shall in no wise pass from the law, till all be fulfilled. [19] Whosoever therefore shall break one of these least commandments, and shall teach men so, he shall be called the least in the kingdom of heaven: but whosoever shall do and teach them, the same shall be called great in the kingdom of heaven. (Matthew 5:17–19)

When we go against the law as it is written, we are clearly sinning and are condemned unless we repent and pray in Jesus's name for forgiveness. It is our God-given duty to share this with those who are ignorant of His Law. We must humbly offer them the way Christ has given us to forgiveness of every repented sin. We are not to judge another. How many times has humility been displaced by fighting over how many angels may fit on the head of a pin?

> [30] Love the Lord your God with all your heart and with all your soul and with all your mind and with all your strength.' [31] The second is this: 'Love your neighbor as yourself.' There is no commandment greater than these." (Mark 12:30–31)

Let us love one another in Jesus Christ as He loves us forever.

A Gift Shared in Love Is Priceless!

The Christmas story *A Christmas Carol* by Charles Dickens describes the transformation of Scrooge, a miserable rich businessman. His counter in this novel is his poorly paid clerk, Bob Cratchit.

Bob barely scrapes by with his wife and five children. Bob's youngest son, Tiny Tim is desperately ill and uses a crutch. Yet Bob was happy, even jolly at Christmas, buoyed by the love his family had in generous supply, made even greater as they shared it with one another in the face of grinding poverty.

Mr. Dickens didn't write *A Christmas Carol* to promote Jesus or Christianity. Dickens was an activist in nineteenth-century London striving to promote his view of the rich elite as heartless and selfish. Dickens used three spirits to school old Scrooge about the value of caring and sharing by scaring Scrooge out of his wits and illustrating the plight of Bob Cratchit whom he oppressed. Scrooge is redeemed when he realizes the terrible error of his ways and selfish philosophy.

In the end, Scrooge shares Christmas with the Cratchit family, providing a great dinner and presents beyond the Cratchits' purse. In return, Scrooge receives a generous share of the love this poor family has in ample supply. Scrooge understands that the love the Cratchits have is far more valuable than all his worth. Each of us can relate to this as we occupy one or more of the characters' places in the story throughout our lives.

The actual Christmas story is true and far more valuable than anything mankind can devise. God descended into our flesh to become the son of Mary who married Joseph, a carpenter. Together, they protected Jesus from harm and shared with Him the love of family. Jesus was a carpenter before He entered His holy ministry to become our risen Lord and Savior who saves everyone who believes in Him and repents of our sins forever.

Being born again in Jesus Christ is the most precious gift, period! Are we Scrooge who would hoard it and hold it for ourselves only? Or are we Bob Cratchit who shared his love and family without hesitation?

When we are adopted into God's own family, we are younger sisters and brothers of Jesus Christ who shares Himself with all who would take His hand. We are saved forever in His love as His Holy Spirit enters our hearts and minds to haunt us with the unending gift of God's love. We grow under His tutoring and understand God's philosophy of sacrificial love.

How can we keep this gift to ourselves? We must share it every Christmas and every day in His most generous Holy Spirit. Let us make everyone rich in Christ so they may join us in His family forever.

Merry Christmas!

> [7] And the peace of God, which transcends all understanding, will guard your hearts and your minds in Christ Jesus. (Philippians 4:7)

A Passing Shower?

The president of the Lutheran Church Missouri Synod, Matthew Harrison, recalled the words of Martin Luther. Martin Luther described the holy gospels as "For you should know that God's Word and grace is like a passing shower of rain which does not return where it has once been."

Martin observed that many nations which embraced the holy gospel and Jesus Christ no longer have Him. They looked to other religions or philosophies to replace Him. Martin Luther, himself a German, said, "And you Germans need not think that you will have it forever, for ingratitude and contempt will not make it stay. Therefore, seize it and hold it fast, whoever can; for lazy hands are bound to have a lean year."

Our republic was founded by men and women fleeing oppression of the gospels. Many in Europe were replacing the Word of God with their own agendas designed to their personal desires.

The Pilgrims planted seeds in our ground to feed themselves in the short and long term. They also built Christian churches to preserve their souls forever. Just as water falling from above nourishes the crops in the ground, the Holy Spirit nourishes the way within us.

America is truly a most blessed nation in natural resources. When we embraced and shared the holy gospel with one another throughout the generations, the colonies flourished and grew. Our ancestors defeated the greatest army and navy on earth to become independent of the king of England. This was done with shed blood and prayerful petitions to God in Jesus's name. Their prayers were answered.

We have always been sinners all. Slavery and our treatment of Native Americans are dark shadows from which we struggle to repent. Still, church steeples abounded, and most Americans attended church faithfully worshipping our Lord and trying to serve Him according the His Word.

What about today? Do we study the gospels? Do we share them with our families? How many attend church regularly? How do our national and local governments treat Christ and His church? Is God's shower of blessings upon us passing? Are we still His faithful Christian nation?

Have we slacked our physical thirst with the abundance of passing pleasures offered by our merchants so that we no longer thirst for the Word of God and salvation? God created Adam and Eve with individual free will. He created you and me with free will too. He loves us beyond our comprehension. He offers salvation, but the choice is ours.

> [16] For God so loved the world that he gave his one and only Son, that whoever believes in him shall not perish but have eternal life. (John 3:16)

Attend church, study the Bible, and feel a thirst for Jesus Christ.

> [6] Jesus saith unto him, I am the way, the truth, and the life: no man cometh unto the Father, but by me. (John 14:6)

Adopted?

I have used "adopted as brothers and sisters" as the description of Christians who have been saved in the blood-shed grace of Jesus Christ.

I believe that we should consider the Jesus's parable of the prodigal son. See Luke 15:11–32 who demanded his inheritance from his father and left to squander his inheritance in wild and sinful living. Before long, the prodigal son is broke and starving, abandoned by his friends who helped him spend his inheritance. In desperate circumstances, the prodigal returns home, intent to plead to become a slave of his father so that he might survive.

> [20] But while he was still a long way off, his father saw him and was filled with compassion for him; he ran to his son, threw his arms around him and kissed him. [21] "The son said to him, 'Father, I have sinned against heaven and against you. I am no longer worthy to be called your son.' [22] "But the father said to his servants, 'Quick! Bring the best robe and put it on him. Put a ring on his finger and sandals on his feet. [23] Bring the fattened calf and kill it. Let's have a feast and celebrate. [24] For this son of mine was dead and is alive again; he was lost and is found.' So they began to celebrate. (Luke 15:20–24)

I believe we are indeed brothers and sisters to Jesus Christ, created by the same Father/God. We are lost in the darkness of sin by our own selfish choices. Jesus tells us, "[9] Pray, then, in this way: Our Father who is in heaven, Hallowed be Your name" (Matthew 6:9).

Jesus Christ is Immanuel. "[14] And the Word was made flesh, and dwelt among us (and we beheld his glory, the glory as of the only begotten of the Father,) full of grace and truth" (John 1:14).

Jesus left our Father to join us in the darkness, lost in sin. "[12] Again Jesus spoke to them, saying, I am the light of the world. Whoever follows me will not walk in darkness, but will have the light of life" (John 8:12).

I believe we are prodigal children of God who are born again by the blood-shed grace of Jesus Christ who prayed to Our Father, "[34]

Then said Jesus, 'Father, forgive them; for they know not what they do'" (Luke 23:34).

When we confess praying for forgiveness in Jesus's name, consider the prodigal son: "[21] The son said to him, Father, I have sinned against heaven and against you. I am no longer worthy to be called your son" (Luke 15:21). We return to the place God has for us in His family. "[6]Jesus saith unto him, I am the way, the truth, and the life: no man cometh unto the Father, but by me" (John 14:6).

Thank you, Jesus! Merry Christmas to all, those are born again in Jesus Christ and those who have not seen His light. Let us share Him always.

All from One, All to One

[1] In the beginning was the Word, and the Word was with God, and the Word was God. [2] He was in the beginning with God. [3] All things came into being through Him, and apart from Him not even one thing came into being that has come into being. (John 1:1–3)

[26] and He made from one man every nation of mankind to live on all the face of the earth. (Acts 17:26)

[14] And the Word was made flesh, and dwelt among us, (and we beheld his glory, the glory as of the only begotten of the Father,) full of grace and truth. (John 1:14)

[6] Jesus saith unto him, I am the way, the truth, and the life: no man cometh unto the Father, but by me. (John 14:6)

[14] Let not your heart be troubled: believe in God, believe also in me. [2] In my Father's house are

many mansions; if it were not so, I would have told you; for I go to prepare a place for you. ³And if I go and prepare a place for you, I come again, and will receive you unto myself; that where I am, there ye may be also. (John 14:1–3)

Nobody Knows!

We live in a hedonistic culture where many of us are convinced of our personal superiority. Secular philosophy celebrates perspectives that are founded on the notion that individual worth and personal desires are our own truths to fashion for ourselves. Furthermore, no other truth is superior to our own. This is rubbish!

This strategy is older than recorded history. It is divide and conquer. Satan used it by convincing Adam and Eve that they must step away from God and eat the forbidden fruit. He convinced them that their Creator knew they were clever individuals whom God feared, not loved. "⁵ For God knows that in the day you eat from it your eyes will be opened, and you will be like God, knowing good and evil" (Genesis 3:5).

Jesus experienced the perspective of flesh and blood from His humble birth to His bitter suffering and death on the cross. Those who are born again in Him receive the holy gift of salvation, and we begin to experience His perspective. Jesus knows every heart.

Mahalia Jackson, perhaps the most powerful gospel singer ever, released this song in 1960.

> Nobody knows the trouble I've seen
> Nobody knows but He knows my sorrow
> Yes, nobody knows the trouble I've seen
> But glory, Hallelujah
>
> Sometimes I'm standing crying
> Tears running down my face
> I cry to the Lord, have mercy
> Help me run this all race

Oh Lord, I have so many trials
So many pains and woes

I'm asking for faith and comfort
Lord, help me to carry this load, whoo

Nobody knows the trouble I've seen
Well, no, nobody knows but Jesus
No nobody knows, oh the trouble, the trouble
　　I've seen
I'm singing glory, glory, glory, Hallelujah

No nobody knows, oh the trouble, the trouble
　　I've seen
Lord, no nobody knows my sorrow
No nobody knows, you know the trouble The
trouble I've seen
I'm singing glory, glory, glory, Hallelujah!

Let us pray that those who celebrate their isolation may break down the walls they constructed to join us in Jesus Christ forever. We must share Him with them. He is their only hope!

Blissfully Lost

There are very different states of mind and soul. We all know this. We are occasionally reminded that our state of mind is not always appropriate to the circumstances in which we find ourselves. As loving parents, we carefully watch our babies as they grow into young children (and truth be known even when they are adults) so that we can shield them from the consequences of bad decisions. It's simple at first, "Don't touch that it will burn you!"

As they become more self-aware and confident (they know everything), we find ourselves in a struggle to protect them. "I am so tired of you interfering with my life!" "Just leave me alone!" (that would be adolescence).

Even as we are there for them as they make the same mistakes we did, it seems a losing battle. Their adult choices can be life-ending or self-destructive to horrible degrees. A broken heart from a bad relationship may be replaced by a heart that no longer beats due to overdose, accidents, or crime. Our hearts break for them in desperate frustration, as they refuse to listen.

Through it all, they often remain convinced that "I'll be fine if you just leave me alone!" right up to the moment it isn't fine at all. Sometimes, we experience the unthinkable. We watch as he or she slips away in death forever.

God, our Father, feels this for every one of us. He created each of us. "[16] For God so loved the world, that he gave his only begotten Son, that whosoever believeth on him should not perish, but have eternal life (John 3:16).

We are lemmings rushing over the cliff into the sea of eternal darkness until someone shares the blessed light of Jesus Christ through the Word of God with us. Oblivious in our ignorance, we deny anything is wrong as satan constantly works to hide God's Word and the salvation available only through Jesus Christ, from us. "[6] Jesus saith unto him, I am the way, and the truth, and the life: no one cometh unto the Father, but by me". (John 14:6).

Please, let us share the Word of God and the blood-shed grace of Jesus Christ with everyone, always. There is no greater light. There is no greater gift. There is no other way. There is only the way Jesus Christ gave His life to make for us. May we and others with whom we share Him leave our secular adolescence in the darkness behind us to walk in His light forever.

Let us give Jesus Christ God's greatest gift for Christmas! He is indeed "the Gift that keeps on giving" forever!

All of Us Equal, All

"We hold these truths to be self-evident, that all men are created equal, that they are endowed by their Creator with certain unalienable Rights, that among these are Life, Liberty and the pursuit of Happiness"—the Declaration of Independence from the king of

England, adopted by the thirteen colonies on July 4, 1776, begins with these words.

The self-evident Truth to which they ascribed unanimously is found first in the Word of God. They give God the credit due on this point in the previous paragraph.

This self-evident Truth was evident to the men and women of the colonies and across the world because they shared Jesus Christ and the Holy Bible. The closer our nation held to Jesus, the more God's richest blessings rained down upon our hearts to cultivate a mutually held love that strengthened the roots of our Tree of Liberty. Men and women of every status strove together to defeat the world's strongest army fielded by the king of England. Few bet on the colonies to prevail. But prevail they did, according to God's will.

Thomas Jefferson wrote these words in a letter he penned in 1787, "The tree of liberty must be refreshed from time to time with the blood of patriots and tyrants." He recognized that our revolutionary victory was always to be under attack as our republic was founded on God's Word.

On the last day of the Constitutional Convention, September 18, 1787, "A lady asked Dr. (Benjamin) Franklin, 'Well, Doctor, what have we got a republic or a monarchy?' 'A republic,' replied the doctor, 'if you can keep it.'"

Jesus Christ set the stage for this noble declaration of equality as He ministered to us in our flesh. [Jesus said] "Then the righteous will answer Him saying, 'Lord, when did we see You hungry and feed You or thirsty and give You drink? And when did we see You a stranger and welcome You or naked and clothe You? And when did we see You sick or in prison and visit You?' And the King will answer them, 'Truly I say to you, as you did it to one of the least of these, My brothers, you did it to Me'" (Matthew 25:37–40).

Jesus's blood-shed grace is offered to everyone regardless of their status in our flesh. Jesus paid particular attention and love to those who we would cast as the least of us. "Truly I say to you, as you did it to one of the least of these, My brothers, you did it to Me" (Matthew 25:40).

May we pay particular care and attention to those who have the least. We enjoy endless love and unending mercy in Jesus Christ, as they do also. Let us share ourselves and our treasure as Jesus shares His shed blood to wash us all clean of the filth of our sins.

Beyond Imagination!

I remember being told that there are no limits to imagination. Walt Disney took this to heart and created the largest entertainment company in America. He founded Walt Disney Imagineering Research and Development, Inc. It is the research and development arm of the Walt Disney Company.

Disney organized an incredibly sophisticated and complex collection of people, places, and organizations dedicated to the creativity of human imagination.

As impressive as it seems to us, it is in truth simply repeating plots and stories using varying characters, settings, and costumes. Shakespeare wrote nothing new. He paints the canvass with brighter colors, richer words, and unexpected twists, with great imagination.

Everything we imagine is formed within the perspective of our flesh. Many of us resort to drugs to seek something new that may pleasure us in ways beyond our imagination. Others travel endlessly, seeking something new and different for the same reason. There are many ways to see something new and different.

God our Creator in Heaven, God our Savior in Jesus Christ, and God our Comforter in the Holy Spirit are beyond our imaginations because they are beyond our flesh. As Jesus told Pilate, "[36] My kingdom is not of this world. If it were, my servants would fight to prevent my arrest by the Jewish leaders. But now my kingdom is from another place" (John 18:36).

Jesus descended from Heaven into the perspective of our flesh through His birth to the Virgin Mary. He lived a perfectly innocent life without a sin of any kind to become that perfect, final sacrifice for us. Jesus told His disciples, "[19] Before long, the world will not see me anymore, but you will see me. Because I live, you also will live.

²⁰ On that day you will realize that I am in my Father, and you are in me, and I am in you" (John 14:19–20). Jesus speaks to us from a spiritual perspective that is beyond this flesh.

It is faith in Him and the Word of God that saves and sustains us because we cannot imagine His perspective. Whatever we cannot understand, whatever may not seem to make sense to us as we read His Word is no less true. It is beyond our understanding within our perspective of the flesh.

> ⁶ Be anxious for nothing, but in everything by prayer and supplication with thanksgiving let your requests be made known to God. ⁷ And the peace of God, which surpasses all comprehension, will guard your hearts and your minds in Christ Jesus. (Philippians 4:6–7)

Let not your imagination constrain you from faith in Jesus Christ. He is beyond our imagination, until He brings us home to Him when our flesh releases our imprisoned spirit. I pray we will share eternity together in Him.

Beyond Olympians

The Apostle Paul compared the discipline necessary to compete in the ancient Greek athletic games with our lives as Christians who are saved by the blood-shed grace of Jesus Christ.

> ²⁴ Do you not know that in a race all the runners run, but only one gets the prize? Run in such a way as to get the prize. ²⁵ Everyone who competes in the games goes into strict training. They do it to get a crown that will not last, but we do it to get a crown that will last forever. (1 Corinthians 9:24–25)

Paul went on to use himself as an example of the discipline required of Christians, who must also discipline our bodies as we seek to behave as God wishes.

> [26] Therefore I do not run like someone running aimlessly; I do not fight like a boxer beating the air. [27] No, I strike a blow to my body and make it my slave so that after I have preached to others, I myself will not be disqualified for the prize. (1 Corinthians 9:26–27)

We devote ourselves to Jesus Christ who laid down every comfort, suffered every pain, and died for every sin so that we may be adopted into God's heavenly family as brothers and sisters in Jesus. Sometimes, we may hear that all we need do is accept Jesus as our risen Lord and Savior and repent of our sin in His holy name to be saved forever. Some may believe that once you do that, you don't have to do anything more. Salvation is not a Get Out of Jail Free card eternally. Again, we listen to Paul:

> [13] Brothers and sisters, I do not consider myself yet to have taken hold of it. But one thing I do: Forgetting what is behind and straining toward what is ahead, [14] I press on toward the goal to win the prize for which God has called me heavenward in Christ Jesus. (Philippians 3:13–14)

Accepting the blood-shed grace of Jesus Christ does give us forgiveness of every sin. Loving Him as He loves us changes our spiritual relationship for the good forever. Sadly, we continue to sin in this flesh and will do so until we breathe our last. The salvation difference is that we no longer celebrate our sins or the momentary pleasure they may bring us. We regret them and the pain Christ endured on the cross for each one we commit.

The indwelling Holy Spirit is our eternal life coach. He sets us on the way of Jesus and accompanies us as we "press on toward the goal to win the prize for which God has called me heavenward in Christ Jesus" (Philippians 3:14).

May we celebrate the greatest gift of all this Christmas, *salvation*! It is the prize we all share as the eternal, loving gift of Jesus Christ. I pray we will always share Him.

Christlike

> [1] See what great love the Father has lavished on us, that we should be called children of God! And that is what we are! The reason the world does not know us is that it did not know him. [2] Dear friends, now we are children of God, and what we will be has not yet been made known. But we know that when Christ appears, we shall be like him, for we shall see him as he is. [3] All who have this hope in him purify themselves, just as he is pure. (1 John 3:1–3)

Truly, we do not know the full nature of Jesus Christ's gift of grace that He has bestowed upon each and every one of us who knows Him as our risen Lord and Savior. Christ's divine nature became clothed in our flesh when He descended from Heaven through Mary's womb.

We read of the miracles, love, grace, and mercy He shared with us. We know this from God's own words at Jesus's baptism: "[17] And a voice from Heaven said, 'This is my Son, whom I love; with him I am well pleased'" (Matthew 3:17).

It is Jesus Christ the man, whom every witness to Him saw or touched or who was touched by Him to experience miraculous healings or holy insights.

Moses came face-to-face with God.

> [29] When Moses came down from Mount Sinai with the two tablets of the covenant law in his hands, he was not aware that his face was radiant because he had spoken with the Lord. [30]

> When Aaron and all the Israelites saw Moses, his face was radiant, and they were afraid to come near him. (Exodus 34:29–30)

Each time Moses went to speak to God, his face would become radiant. Moses began wearing a veil over his face to calm his fellow Jews.

John shares with us what the Holy Spirit shared with him. The angel who appeared before the shepherds at Jesus's birth affirmed Him to be a wonderful gift to us all. "[10] But the angel said to them, 'Do not be afraid. I bring you good news that will cause great joy for all the people'" (Luke 2:10).

Jesus tells us: "[25] Jesus said to her, 'I am the resurrection and the life. The one who believes in me will live, even though they die; [26] and whoever lives by believing in me will never die. Do you believe this?'" (John 11:25–26)

When our flesh fails and releases our spirits reborn into Jesus Christ through the Holy Spirit, we will join Him in His kingdom which is beyond our physical reach or mortal understanding. I believe John has shown us a glimpse of the gift of grace Christ has given us. Thanks be to God that we share that gift!

Come, Lord Jesus!

As children many of us were taught to bless our meals with the prayer that begins, "Come, Lord Jesus." Our family recited it at our dinner tables when modern schedules allowed us all to be around the table together. My bride Janet and I share it at breakfast every morning.

> Come, Lord Jesus, be our guest and let Thy gifts to us be blessed.
> Help us walk with You each day
> and be a blessing to others along The Way

While this blessing is usually said over our meals, it is a simple way to thank God for every blessing He sends us in the name of Jesus Christ. It expresses our desire to be of Jesus Christ, to walk with Him along the way, He gives us through His shed blood. He died so that we may live forever with Him. Finally, it asks Him to help us share Him with the world around as God's richest blessing.

Of course, life in this realm of satan is not without disease, injury, and eventually death for our flesh. None of us awaken to Heaven on earth in every moment of our short lives. Sometimes, our hearts are burdened, and our eyes shed tears in grief or pain.

May we remember these words from Revelation 21:3–4,

> [3] And I heard a loud voice from the throne saying, "Behold, the dwelling place of God is with man. He will dwell with them, and they will be his people, and God himself will be with them as their God. [4] He will wipe away every tear from their eyes, and death shall be no more, neither shall there be mourning, nor crying, nor pain anymore, for the former things have passed away."

We endure in this brief now that seems sometimes to cover us in endless pain or sadness forever. Let us recall that it is indeed brief. At the end of the way Jesus made for us, we will be reunited in Him, in His peace, and His joy forever.

Day of Reckoning

Christians who study the Holy Bible or hear the Word faithfully preached from the pulpit on Sundays are familiar with the circumstances and consequences that come with Jesus in His second coming to us in our flesh.

Christ comes not to teach and preach as He did when He was last with us. Jesus shared Himself with us by teaching, preaching, performing miraculous signs, and rising from death to celebrate the Truth of His victory over satan, sin, and death, for us.

> [25] Jesus said unto her, "I am the resurrection and the Life. He that believeth in Me, though he were dead, yet shall he live; [26] and whosoever liveth and believeth in Me shall never die. Believest thou this?" (John 11:25–26)

God sends the Holy Spirit into the hearts that believe in Jesus Christ. God gives us His Holy Bible to study so we may understand what He expects of us and what we my expect of Jesus Christ, our risen Lord and Savior. "[16] For God so loved the world that He gave His only begotten Son, that whosoever believeth in Him should not perish, but have everlasting life" (John 3:16).

The Bible describes the circumstances that will lead up to His second coming in Jesus's own words (see Matthew 24).

Jesus also tells us what will happens when He comes: "[31] When the Son of Man comes in his glory and all his angels are with him, he will sit on his glorious throne. [32] The people of every nation will be gathered in front of him. He will separate them as a shepherd separates the sheep from the goats" (Matthew 25:31–32).

Many times in the two thousand years since Jesus ascended back to Heaven, people have seen evil rise up and horrific destruction worked among us, by us on one another. They were certain they were witnessing the end-times. They weren't. Jesus spoke to us about his as well: "[36] But of that day and hour no one knows, not even the angels of heaven, but My Father only. [44] Therefore you also be ready, for the Son of Man is coming at an hour you do not expect" (Matthew 24:36, 44).

Until Jesus returns, every one of us has the opportunity to know Him as our risen Lord and Savior. Every one of us who repents in His holy name will be saved, becoming lambs of God. We will not be the goats who do not know Him and are eternally damned.

May we share Jesus with everyone we know and love. May we share him with friends and acquaintances. May we share Him with strangers. This is what He wants us to do so that more may be saved before He returns and it is too late for them.

Thanks be to God that we know Jesus is our risen Lord and Savior.

Death No More

Most of us have visited with a relative, a loved one, or friend who is dying. Sitting alongside their bed, choking back tears and an overwhelming sadness. We are often filled with regret as we consider the time and attention we gave to them before death came to claim them from us.

The death of one we know and love is a defining moment for them and for us. Its definition is formed across a lifetime we shared with them. How many times did we put off visiting them or words we wish we had spoken to them that still haunt us? There is little room for joy it seems.

Yet as I was in the depths of despair at my brother's deathbed, he rose from a deep slumber as his life's energy was depleted over years fighting cancer. It was surprising he was able to regain consciousness. He smiled at me to reassure me! His eyes were brightened by people and things unseen by we healthy ones around him. In what many more intelligent people call delirium, Tommy has been speaking to deceased members of our family in the hours before he passed. He smiled in those moments.

Years later, I was alongside a cousin who was also on her deathbed from disease. She too was lifted in her delirium as she saw things beyond our mortal flesh.

We know Jesus Christ is our risen Lord and Savior who defeated death and waits at our side to bring us to Him eternally. We certainly regret parting from those we come to know and love in our lifetimes shared with them here. But our attitude should not be despair. We know we will join those who have passed over from this flesh in Jesus. We will live forever in "the peace of God which surpasses all understanding" (Philippians 4:7).

Let us not grieve for our brothers and sisters in Jesus Christ who have passed over to His hands. Christian funerals are places of joy for those who are in Heaven and sadness for us who miss them so much. Our tears of loss will change one day to tears of joy as the shock of the loss in our hearts fades and the joy of the eternal reunion that is ahead fills us once again.

Joy to the world, our Lord has come! Joy to Christians for whom He comes again to bring us home as children of God. In that moment as our flesh fails and releases its mortal grip on our spirits, we take Jesus's extended hand.

Father, please help us to focus on the eternal tomorrow you have prepared for us in Jesus, and may we give thanks to you in every circumstance.

Embrace His Light

Some of today's essay comes from one of my first devotions. Many of us have experienced camping out in the woods where the day is full of sun, fun, and adventures. But as evening skies darken, we retreat to gather around the campfire built to provide us light, warmth, and perhaps nourishment cooked over the open fire.

Now, the world around us is now less inviting, even threatening. Who wants to venture alone into the darkness beyond the light? Not me!

Science says our sun won't last forever. The light of Jesus Christ God's only begotten Son will never dim. He is always with us (Matthew 28:20). Let His light and love warm you and keep you for it will never die nor will we who believe in Him and repent of our sins (John 11:26).

Jesus tells us He is coming again in judgment. "[22] Jesus said to His followers, 'The time will come when you will wish you could see the Son of Man for one day. But you will not be able to. [23] They will say to you, "He is here," or, "He is there," but do not follow them. [24] When the Son of Man comes, He will be as lightning that shines from one part of the sky to the other'" (Luke 17:22–24).

SELECTED DEVOTIONS

Christians embrace the light of Christ as the way He formed in His life, death, and resurrection. His light is peace and eternal salvation. We embrace Him in deeply personal love.

> [4] But you, brothers and sisters, are not in darkness, so that the day would overtake you like a thief; [5] for you are all sons of light and sons of day. We are not of night nor of darkness. (1 Thessalonians 5:4–5)

Those who don't know the light of Christ by ignorance or by rejection, dwell in the darkness of sin and death. Let us share Jesus with everyone we can to let His light shine into their darkness. Jesus commands us, "[19] Therefore go and make disciples of all nations, baptizing them in the name of the Father and of the Son and of the Holy Spirit, [20] and teaching them to obey everything I have commanded you" (Matthew 28:19–20).

May we remember these words from the 1954 song, "Open Up Your Heart (And Let the Sunshine In)" by Stuart Hamblen, with a few slight changes.

> So let the sun Son shine in
> Face it Him with a grin
> Open up your heart and let the sun Son shine in.
> When you are unhappy,
> The devil wears a grin
> But oh, he starts to running
> When Christ's light comes pouring in

Thanks be to God for the eternal light of our beloved risen Lord and Savior who will return to ban all darkness and evil forever. We live in His light and love.

Embrace the Darkness?

Psychologists coined the term Stockholm syndrome to describe the actions of some people who feel trapped in abusive circumstances that are beyond their control. It was named after some hostages in a bank robbery in Stockholm, Sweeden, became devoted to those who held them captive.

Police officers were quite familiar with this behavior long before psychologists. It was and sadly remains common when they respond to domestic disturbance calls to the same address repeatedly. It is one of the most dangerous calls for service because as they separate the parties and threaten the aggressor with arrest, the victim may instantly come to his defense even as she is bleeding from his violence. Officers have died at the hands of these reunited couples.

The victim who cried out for protection is convinced that if the aggressor is arrested, she will be worse off when he returns home in a short while. Or that if she leaves him life will be worse than it is with him.

How often have we heard the criticism of Christianity as a fantasy wherein, "They believe an old man with a white beard will magically make everything better." These skeptics seek to demean those with faith because they are trapped in the darkness of secular thinking, promoted by satan. They become devoted to the darkness because it is familiar, and they are convinced there is no light that may penetrate it. They fear any promise of delivery from their present circumstances because they are afraid the promise may be false and just make things worse for them. They embrace the darkness.

[17] So then faith cometh by hearing, and hearing by the word of God. (Romans 10:17)

[14] And the Word was made flesh, and dwelt among us (and we beheld his glory, the glory as of the only begotten of the Father) full of grace and truth. (John 1:14)

> [8] For it is by grace you have been saved, through faith—and this is not from yourselves, it is the gift of God— [9] not by works, so that no one can boast. (Ephesians 2:8–9)

> [12] Again Jesus spoke to them, saying, "I am the light of the world. Whoever follows me will not walk in darkness, but will have the light of life." (John 8:12)

The prophet Isaiah tells of God's attention to our prayers, "[24] And it shall come to pass, that before they call, I will answer; and while they are yet speaking, I will hear" (Isaiah 65:24) May we answer the unspoken plea for His grace from those who know Him not. Let us answer it with faith in the Word made flesh who is our eternal light. We may not see success in every offer of Jesus Christ to those who have no faith but pray they may glimpse His light in their darkness and begin walking along the way He created for everyone, in faith.

Enemies of satan

> [16] For God so loved the world that he gave his one and only Son, that whoever believes in him shall not perish but have eternal life. (John 3:16)

As Jesus stood before Pontious Pilate, Pilate asked Him, "Are you the king of the Jews?" (John 18:33). "[36] Jesus answered, 'My kingdom is not of this world. If My kingdom were of this world, My servants would be fighting so that I would not be handed over to the Jews; but as it is, My kingdom is not of this realm'" (John 18:36).

We are condemned by the original sin of Adam and Eve. Our natural inclination is toward sin and death. Every imperfection in our corrupt world originates with their sin. "[8] Be sober, be watchful: your adversary the devil, as a roaring lion, walketh about, seeking whom he may devour" (1 Peter 5:8). Satan doesn't force anyone to submit to him. He persuades us to follow our sinful inclinations. Satan did not touch the whips that tore Jesus's flesh before He was nailed to the cross. He did not drive a nail.

It is we who choose which path to follow. The fatal road satan offers is an attractive highway that accommodates our rush to death. The greater the number of doomed souls, the wider the highway. Satan doesn't want us to slow down in the ever-increasing traffic lest we have time to consider and exit on the ramp Jesus Christ offers. Jesus is the way to eternal life in peace. In Matthew's Gospel, we read, "[13] Enter by the narrow gate. For the gate is wide and the way is easy that leads to destruction, and those who enter by it are many. [14] For the gate is narrow and the way is hard that leads to life, and those who find it are few" (Matthew 7:13–14).

Those who know Jesus as their personal Risen Lord and Savior choose the way He created for us from His shed blood. We attract special, focused attention from satan. It was satan who misled all who conspired to betray and murder Jesus. God's innocent Son who died for our sins. Jesus used death to enter hell to defeat satan, sin, and death forever for us. "[25] Jesus said to her, 'I am the resurrection and the life. The one who believes in me will live, even though they die; [26] and whoever lives by believing in me will never die. Do you believe this?'" (John 11:25–26).

Satan targets Christians with all manner of pain and grief as he attempts to change our minds. Jesus tells us, "[28] I give them eternal life, and they shall never perish; no one will snatch them out of my hand" (John 10:28).

May this holy season refresh our love for Him and one another in Him. May it strengthen our faith in Him. "And lo, I am with you always, even unto the end of the world." Amen. Merry Christmas!

Understanding His Peace

"You're not the boss of me!" is a childhood phrase that resonates with humor and love within our family. We retell the story of our youngest granddaughter. She put her hands on her hips and stared up at Grandma to forcefully make this pronouncement. The others gathered around her at Camp Grandma were silently stunned and sure she was about to experience a life-changing moment when Grandma corrected her. Grandma took a breath and laughed. That little rebel is now in college. She is a bright and beautiful young woman whom we love dearly, as we do every one of them.

Yet that declaration of independence reveals a most serious problem with our human nature. It fractures individual, familial, corporate, and international relationships. Today, some exploit this to sew chaos, violence, and destruction in our homes, on our streets, and across our borders.

We are advised never to speak of politics or religion if we wish to keep our friends. Yet this is exactly what we must discuss if we are to be born-again children of God through Jesus Christ.

Jesus told the Pharisees Nicodemus, "[36] He that believeth on the Son hath everlasting life: and he that believeth not the Son shall not see life; but the wrath of God abideth on him" (John 3:36). This declaration comes from the Word made flesh (John 1:14); the only begotten Son of God (John 3:16). It is black or white, light or darkness. there are no shades of gray.

God, our heavenly Father, wishes every one of us to become His sons or daughters through Jesus Christ. "[6] Jesus saith unto him, I am the way, the truth, and the life: no man cometh unto the Father, but by me" (John 14:6).

Jesus does not wish to force us into submission. He prayed to His Father from the cross, "[34] Then Jesus said, 'Father, forgive them, for they do not know what they do'" (Luke 23:34).

God sent His Son Jesus Christ to save us, not condemn us. It is only when we know Him and choose to be as He wishes that, we are born again sharing the Word of God. We return His loving embrace and making no declaration that "You're not the boss of me!" He is our King, our Father, and our Savior. We pray to please Him and be instruments of His divine will. Accepting His perfect wisdom, "[7] and the peace of God, which surpasses all understanding, will guard your hearts and minds through Christ Jesus (Philippians 4:7).

Thanks be to God!

No! Entitled!

We still have the original Declaration of Independence which began our separation from the king of England and the Constitution which describes the republic we shaped to replace that relationship of dependence.

Our Declaration of Independence was drafted by Christians who saw Jesus Christ as the cornerstone of every good thing. "We, therefore, the Representatives of the United States of America, in General Congress, Assembled, appealing to the Supreme Judge of the world for the rectitude of our intentions." These are the first words of the Declaration of Independence.

What was the context of this Declaration to Christians? It was obvious to them as they studied the unchanging Word of God in the Bible. We find the following description of Jesus in Revelation 19:16, "^{16} On his robe and on his thigh he has this name written: King of Kings and Lord of Lords." They declared our independence of every earthly king.

More familiar than the first sentence of the Declaration are these words: "We hold these Truths to be self-evident, that all Men are created equal, that they are endowed by their Creator with certain unalienable Rights, that among these are Life, Liberty, and the Pursuit of Happiness" (emphasis added). Our Christian founders declared that God endows us with gifts He provides to pursue happiness within His creation.

We are equally helpless newborns when we emerge from our mother's womb. Yet each of us is endowed with gifts from God to see us through our brief lives in this flesh. God gives us each our own free will. He also endows us with other gifts we may use for ourselves and, more importantly, for others on our sojourn here.

God gives us the opportunity to study His Word to be saved in Jesus Christ. "^{8} For it is by grace you have been saved, through faith—and this is not from yourselves, it is the gift of God—^{9} not by works, so that no one can boast" (Ephesians 2:8–9).

And what is the source of faith? "So then faith cometh by hearing, and hearing by the Word of God" (Romans 10:17). No one is entitled to anything. How we use the free will He gives us while exercising every other gift He gives us becomes the steps we take along the path we choose in this flesh?

May we pray for everyone who doesn't know Jesus, pray that we may share Jesus with everyone so that no one may remain ignorant of Him. "[6] Jesus saith unto him, I am the way, the truth, and the life: no man cometh unto the Father, but by me" (John 14:6).

He commands us, "[19] Go ye therefore, and make disciples of all the nations, baptizing them into the name of the Father and of the Son and of the Holy Spirit: [20] teaching them to observe all things whatsoever I commanded you: and lo, I am with you always, even unto the end of the world" (Matthew 28:19–20).

What of the Boy?

The Bible is nearly silent on the childhood of Jesus Christ. It is a mystery that confounds secularist researchers and leaves the faithful wishing we knew more of our risen Lord and Savior. How could the childhood of God dwelling in our flesh go unrecorded?

God has not revealed it to us for His own reasons. I find the verses recounting Jesus's return to His hometown particularly interesting when I think about this.

> [53] When Jesus had finished these parables, He departed from there. [54] He came to His hometown and began teaching them in their synagogue, so that they were astonished, and said, "Where did this man get this wisdom and these miraculous powers? [55] Is not this the carpenter's son? Is not His mother called Mary, and His brothers, James and Joseph and Simon and Judas? [56] And His sisters, are they not all with us? Where then did this man get all these things?" [57] And they took offense at Him. But Jesus said to them, "A prophet is not without honor except in his hometown and in his own household." [58] And

> He did not do many miracles there because of their unbelief. (Matthew 13:53–58)

Perhaps the phrase "Familiarity breeds contempt" may apply here. We see Jesus Christ as the Word made flesh (see John 1:14), in the full context of His life, death, resurrection, and ascension back to His Father in Heaven.

Jesus tells us, "⁸ For it is by grace you have been saved, through faith—and this is not from yourselves, it is the gift of God—⁹ not by works, so that no one can boast" (Ephesians 2:8–9).

A Roman centurion sent servants to ask Jesus to heal his servant who was dying,

> ⁶ So Jesus went with them. He was not far from the house when the centurion sent friends to say to him: "Lord, don't trouble yourself, for I do not deserve to have you come under my roof. ⁷ That is why I did not even consider myself worthy to come to you. But say the word, and my servant will be healed. ⁹ When Jesus heard this, he was amazed at him, and turning to the crowd following him, he said, "I tell you, I have not found such great faith even in Israel." ¹⁰ Then the men who had been sent returned to the house and found the servant well. (Luke 7:6–7 and 9–10)

When a woman who was ill reached out and touched Jesus's robe, He felt her presence.

> ³⁴ And He said to her, "Daughter, your faith has made you well. Go in peace, and be healed of your affliction." (Mark 5:34)

Satan attempts to make us too familiar with God so that our knowledge may breed contempt and doom us forever. I pray, Father, in Jesus's name that we will faithfully live in awe of your power and majesty without doubt or condition. Thanks be to God!

Faith Equals Salvation

Jesus's nail-scarred hand is extended to you without fail in every circumstance. We have but to reach out to Him in faith to accept His blood-shed gift of grace, eternal.

Recently, a treasured friend, Pastor Manuel Rivera, posted a message on Facebook in which he recounted Peter stepping out from a boat he was riding in during a storm. He saw Jesus walking on the water toward him in the gale. Jesus said to Peter, "[29] 'Come,' he said. Then Peter got down out of the boat, walked on the water and came toward Jesus. [30] But when he saw the wind, he was afraid and, beginning to sink, cried out, 'Lord, save me!' [31] Immediately Jesus reached out his hand and caught him. 'You of little faith,' he said, 'why did you doubt?'" (Matthew 14:29–31).

We dwell in this broken world with our sinful natures. Sometimes, storms distract us from our faith in Jesus. Does that doom us forever? Not if we turn our hearts and minds back to Christ who always extends His hand which we let go in doubt.

Simon Peter heard our Lord say this on the night Christ was betrayed.

> [31] "Simon, Simon, behold, Satan demanded to have you, that he might sift you like wheat, [32] but I have prayed for you that your faith may not fail. And when you have turned again, strengthen your brothers." [33] Peter said to him, "Lord, I am ready to go with you both to prison and to death." [34] Jesus said, "I tell you, Peter, the rooster will not crow this day, until you deny three times that you know me." (Luke 22:31–34)

> Peter was challenged three times as people recognized Peter as an associate of Jesus. [59] And

> after an interval of about an hour still another insisted, saying, "Certainly this man also was with him, for he too is a Galilean." [60] But Peter said, "Man, I do not know what you are talking about." And immediately, while he was still speaking, the rooster crowed. [61] And the Lord turned and looked at Peter. And Peter remembered the saying of the Lord, how he had said to him, "Before the rooster crows today, you will deny me three times." [62] And he went out and wept bitterly. (Luke 22:59–62)

Let us take heart as we read Jesus's words in Matthew 16:18, "[18] And I tell you that you are, Peter, and on this rock I will build my church, and the gates of Hades will not overcome it."

Jesus's love for us is rock solid. His light is unwavering. His peace is beyond our understanding.

Turn always back to Christ. He will never deny you. His faith in us never falters.

Evil Free Will

The slaughter of all male babies two years old or younger by King Herod is horrible. Herod ordered this in an attempt to kill the baby Jesus who is our risen Lord and Savior.

This historical event surely provokes the question so often repeated in the face of evil actions against innocents, "Why does God allow this?" When God fashioned man from the dust, He gave Adam free will. This is most Godlike.

As we look through the Old Testament, we read again and again where God or His angels or prophets share the Word of God so that the subjects of this attention might be convinced to follow God's wishes. It is our free will that separates us from every other creature shaped in God's hands at creation.

If God stripped Herod of his free will to stop the slaughter, would Herod still be human? Take this a step further. If God stripped all of us our free will, could we initiate anything good or bad? We are not inanimate dolls. God does not take our free will.

It became abundantly clear that we cannot exercise our free will in accordance with God's Word. No one ever did. We choose sin, even when we don't wish it. The Apostle Paul wrote this to the congregations in Rome, "[15] I do not understand what I do. For what I want to do I do not do, but what I hate I do. And if I do what I do not want to do, I agree that the law is good" (Romans 7:15–16).

Alone, we are helpless against sin and satan. We cannot free ourselves, but God will not take our free will from us. The Babe of Bethlehem is our salvation. "[16] For God so loved the world that he gave his one and only Son, that whoever believes in him shall not perish but have eternal life" (John 3:16).

Before Jesus left us to return to Heaven, He said, "[26] But the Helper, the Holy Spirit, whom the Father will send in My name, He will teach you all things, and bring to your remembrance all things that I said to you" (John 14:26).

May we study His Word so we may learn this transforming lesson: "[8] For it is by grace you have been saved, through faith—and this is not from yourselves, it is the gift of God—[9] not by works, so that no one can boast" (Ephesians 2:8–9).

May we study His Word diligently so that we will seek salvation in Jesus Christ's shed blood which is grace that flows without end. Let us look to the light of Christ to lead from the darkness in which we dwell without Him.

Faith Over Flesh

God's choice of Mary to have His Son began with a frightening encounter with His angel, Gabriel to her. He appeared out of nowhere.

> [30] The angel said to her, "Don't be afraid, Mary; God has shown you his grace. [31] Listen! You will become pregnant and give birth to a son, and you will name him Jesus. [32] He will be great

> and will be called the Son of the Most High. The Lord God will give him the throne of King David, his ancestor. ³³ He will rule over the people of Jacob forever, and his kingdom will never end." (Luke 1:30–33)

When Mary asked how this could be. She was a virgin.

> ³⁵ The angel said to Mary, "The Holy Spirit will come upon you, and the power of the Most High will cover you. For this reason the baby will be holy and will be called the Son of God." ³⁸ Mary said, "I am the servant of the Lord. Let this happen to me as you say!" Then the angel went away. (Luke 1:35, 38)

This brief encounter would change Mary's life forever in ways she could not know. Yet Mary accepted what the Lord said without reservation. What an amazing servant of God. She and her family would become the particular focus of satan as he tried to stop Jesus.

Late in her pregnancy, she and Joseph traveled ninety miles to register for a Roman census. She would give birth in Bethlehem. Herod, the Roman governor over Bethlehem, would order all children two years old and younger to be slain in his attempt to end Jesus.

These were satan's earliest efforts to defeat God as God fulfilled His prophecy in the garden of Eden: "¹⁵ And I will put enmity Between you and the woman, And between your seed and her Seed; He shall bruise your head, And you shall bruise His heel" (Genesis 3:15).

Mary could not know what lay ahead. Everything she did, she did in faith. We have the blessing of knowing her entire story and much more as we study God's Word. There are only two sides: Jesus Christ and satan. We have the opportunity to choose Jesus and to be saved forever as children of God. The choice is ours. Sadly, if we do not choose Jesus, satan takes us.

Just as Mary and Joseph met every challenge in faith, so did Jesus. In Gethsemane, Jesus prayed, "^{39} Going a little farther, he fell with his face to the ground and prayed, 'My Father, if it is possible, may this cup be taken from me. Yet not as I will, but as you will'" (Matthew 26:39).

May we pray to keep our faith in Jesus Christ as we face satan's unending effort to claim us for himself by discouraging us, confusing us, and convincing us there is no God. May we travel the way to our heavenly home that Jesus created in His shed blood.

Fear No Evil

How can we reach a place where we fear no evil? A path often chosen is strength. We may build our bodies through hours of exercise as we eat that which is healthy and train in martial arts. This will surely increase our ability to defend ourselves from those who would attack us hand to hand.

But what of those who come at us with weapons? We may purchase defensive gear like ballistic vests, armored vehicles, or bomb shelters. We must also consider offensive weapons to equal us to those who would use knives, guns, or other instruments of destruction.

Yet even when equipped with the best weapons and defenses as part of the strongest armies or police departments, I assure you that fear is present in the jungles or streets we patrol or simply inhabit.

Fear may confront us in public places or at the noise we hear when we are alone at home. Adrenaline may flood our hearts and minds when strangers or loved ones disagree with passion that seems to be just short of violence.

No one gets out of our lives in this flesh alive! If you believe this, you must experience fear constantly as you struggle to distract yourself from the end. Unvanquished fear is at the root of so many terrible thoughts and behaviors that harm us and others. Those who don't know Jesus are doomed to a frightening end by their unforgiven sins.

King David penned this psalm which explains why Christians can look beyond the evil which surrounds us here, some one thousand years before Christ was born.

> [23] The Lord is my shepherd; I shall not want.
> [2] He maketh me to lie down in green pastures: he leadeth me beside the still waters.
> [3] He restoreth my soul: he leadeth me in the paths of righteousness for his name's sake.
> [4] Yea, though I walk through the valley of the shadow of death, I will fear no evil: for thou art with me; thy rod and thy staff they comfort me.
> [5] Thou preparest a table before me in the presence of mine enemies: thou anointest my head with oil; my cup runneth over.
> [6] Surely goodness and mercy shall follow me all the days of my life: and I will dwell in the house of the Lord for ever. (Psalm 23)

I certainly have experienced fear and continue to do so from time to time as circumstances warrant. We don't look forward to pain or suffering. But in Jesus, we can draw strength and His peace to see us through anything this world we have corrupted with our sins may throw at us. As Jesus tells us, "[25] Jesus said to her, 'I am the resurrection and the life. The one who believes in me will live, even though they die; [26] and whoever lives by believing in me will never die. Do you believe this?'" (John 11:25–26).

In Him, through Him, and with Him "[6] Certainly goodness and faithfulness will follow me all the days of my life, And my dwelling will be in the house of the Lord forever" (Psalm 23).

As our spirits are released from our failed flesh, Jesus guides us home to Him forever.

Firstborn

The firstborn in the Old Testament has a special and continuing meaning. The firstborn son inherited a preeminent place in the family. He has the birthright above any younger brother or sister. He was given greater responsibility and authority.

Who is Jesus Christ? This is critical to Christianity across its denominations. In the 325th year after His death and resurrection, representatives across the world met in Nicea to discuss this. They published the Nicene Creed that is used across Christendom today. You may want to look up the Nicene Creed to read this agreement about our Triune God.

The portion of the Creed that describes Jesus Christ begins:

> "And in one Lord Jesus Christ, the only-begotten Son of God, begotten of His Father before all worlds, God of God, Light of Light, very God of very God, begotten, not made, being of one substance with the Father, by whom all things were made."

This is something we should consider as we read John 3:16, "[16] For God so loved the world that he gave his one and only Son, that whoever believes in him shall not perish but have eternal life." God shares Himself with us through Jesus. Jesus loves us so much that He gave Himself over to the bitter suffering and death on the cross in our hands. As he suffered, He prayed. "[34] Then Jesus said, 'Father, forgive them, for they do not know what they do'" (Luke 23:34).

Jesus's words went beyond simple forgiveness. As He hung on the cross, every sin from across time came upon Him. From Eden to His second coming, they came upon His shoulders there. My every sin and yours as well traveled to Him then and there.

Grace flowed from Jesus's side as His blood. Let us look at the verses before and after John 3:16 for their salvation context.

> [15] That whosoever believeth in him should not perish, but have eternal life.
>
> [16] For God so loved the world, that he gave his only begotten Son, that whosoever believeth in him should not perish, but have everlasting life.
>
> [17] For God sent not his Son into the world to condemn the world; but that the world through him might be saved. (John 3:15–17)

"Born again." This means we are not adopted children in God's family. Through Jesus Christ, we are "born again" into His family. Thanks be to God in Jesus Christ forever and ever!

Firstfruits

Today's devotion explores the firstfruits as explained in the New Testament. Jesus Christ is the firstfruits of salvation. We read in 1 Corinthians 15:20–26:

> [20] But now hath Christ been raised from the dead, the first-fruits of them that are asleep. [21] For since by man came death, by man came also the resurrection of the dead. [22] For as in Adam all die, so also in Christ shall all be made alive. [23] But each in his own order: Christ the first-fruits; then they that are Christ's, at his coming. [24] Then cometh the end, when he shall deliver up the kingdom to God, even the Father; when he shall have abolished all rule and all authority and power. [25] For he must reign, till he hath put all his enemies under his feet. [26] The last enemy that shall be abolished is death.

There is no doubt that our spirits are eternal even as our flesh is fleeting. The spirits of those in Jesus, whose flesh has failed will join

Him in Heaven until Christ returns in His second coming. When Christ returns to establish His kingdom on earth and to deliver His kingdom up to God, those who died in Jesus shall be raised. There spirits will dwell in new bodies as children of God in Jesus Christ. Thank be to God the Father, God the Son, and God the Holy Spirit.

Below are a collection of biblical readings I found on Facebook. After reading the citations attached to each statement, I want to share them with you for consideration. I find reassuring comfort and hope from them. I hope you will too.

After a Believer Dies

Angels usher your soul to Heaven. (Luke 16:22)

You immediately enter God's presence. (2 Corinthians 5:6–8)

You are conscious, thinking, feeling, speech, and memories. (Luke 16:19–31)

You worship with angels and believers before the throne of God and Christ. (Revelations 4:5)

You are aware to some degree of activities and events on Earth. (Revelation 6:9–10)

You recognize and communicate with believers who preceded you to Heaven. (Luke 9:28–36)

Listen Prayerfully

Raising prayers to God in Jesus's name is a frequent and positive decision in and of itself. Paul wrote this:

> ²³ but we preach Christ crucified, to Jews a stumbling block and to Gentiles foolishness, ²⁴ but to those who are the called, both Jews and Greeks, Christ the power of God and the wisdom of God. ²⁵ Because the foolishness of God is wiser than men, and the weakness of God is stronger than men. (1 Corinthians 1:23–25)

Where can I find His voice to guide me? The prophet Elijah fled in fear of his life after threats against him for doing God's work. He went to Horeb, the Mount of God, seeking direction and protection. There, Elijah hid in a cave and sought God's counsel.

> ¹¹ And he said, Go forth, and stand upon the mount before the Lord. And, behold, the Lord passed by, and a great and strong wind rent the mountains, and brake in pieces the rocks before the Lord; but the Lord was not in the wind: and after the wind an earthquake; but the Lord was not in the earthquake: ¹² And after the earthquake a fire; but the Lord was not in the fire: and after the fire a still small voice. (1 Kings 19:11–12)

Elijah did not have Jesus Christ, the Word made flesh, as we do. Let us bear in mind not to let that which seems cataclysmic distract us from our risen Lord and Savior in our times of need. Before Christ ascended back to Heaven, He told us, "[26] But the Comforter, which is the Holy Ghost, whom the Father will send in my name, he shall teach you all things, and bring all things to your remembrance, whatsoever I have said unto you" (John 14:26).

The more we learn from Jesus, the greater His peace becomes in our hearts. He takes the greatest share of our burdens upon Himself.

> "[28] Come to me, all you who are weary and burdened, and I will give you rest. [29] Take my yoke upon you and learn from me, for I am gentle and humble in heart, and you will find rest for your souls. [30] For my yoke is easy and my burden is light." (Matthew 11:28–30)

The New Testament of the Bible reveals God's wisdom He has shared with us through His Son and Holy Spirit. It is the textbook of life in Christ. I pray that the prayers we offer up to God are informed by Jesus Christ and the Holy Spirit as we study His Word in the Bible. A great share of His peace is learning to accept God's will in faith. He answers prayers in His wisdom, not ours. In God we trust. In Him, we rest forever.

Unfailing Foundation

Many who deny Jesus and belittle our faith proudly declare they are critical thinkers. They never rely on hearsay or declarations unsupported by facts they can observe, consider, and weigh to prove which is offered. That is rubbish! One cannot live without faith.

For more than a century our little church in Cumberland, Maryland, has stood at Jesus's house. Then, we decided to repaint the sanctuary and discovered that the foundation on one side of the church was failing. The exterior wall was cracking, and the balcony was separated from the walls to which it was anchored. Until the moment we began to investigate the soundness of the building, we took it for granted. It was a routine matter of faith we must all take to live and function in our world of flesh.

When we opened the floor to inspect it, we discovered it was simply river stones stacked one upon another to form the foundation. This was the standard nearly two hundred years ago, and it worked perfectly until the roots of a tree planted outside the church grew to insinuate themselves between the stones.

It took tons of specially formulated concrete to reinforce the foundation and restore it. The tree has been removed, and everything is safe and sound again.

Even the most skeptical among us walk through life taking for granted that the buildings they access are safe, that the bridges across chasms or rivers are sound, and thousands of other assumptions upon which they place their lives. "Taken for granted" is just another way of saying, "I have faith."

Those who deride our faith as the crutch ride through life blissfully unaware of the wheelchair that carries them. Christians know Jesus Christ is our risen Lord and Savior after studying the Word of God and testimonies of countless generations that have interacted with God through His angels, His prophets, and His only Son, Jesus Christ.

Have I seen Jesus Christ? No. Here is what He says to us who believe in Him.

> [29] Jesus said to him, "Thomas, because you have seen Me, you have believed. Blessed are those who have not seen and yet have believed." (John 20:29)

> [6] Jesus saith unto him, I am the way, the truth, and the life: no man cometh unto the Father, but by me. (John 14:6)

> [25] Jesus said to her, "I am the resurrection and the life. The one who believes in me will

live, even though they die; ²⁶ and whoever lives by believing in me will never die. Do you believe this?" (John 11:25–26)

> ⁸ For it is by grace you have been saved, through faith—and this is not from yourselves, it is the gift of God—⁹ not by works, so that no one can boast. (Ephesians 2:8–9)

Our faith is built upon Jesus Christ, "²² The stone which the builders rejected Has become the chief cornerstone" (Psalm 118:22). Thanks be to God!

Foolish Wisdom

> ¹⁹ For the wisdom of this world is foolishness with God. For it is written, He taketh the wise in their own craftiness. (1 Corinthians 3:19)

Our pursuit of that which we believe to be wisdom is a fool's errand. This is biblical. "¹⁷ But of the tree of the knowledge of good and evil, thou shalt not eat of it: for in the day that thou eatest thereof thou shalt surely die" (Genesis 2:17). These are God's words to Adam and Eve in the garden of Eden. Adam and Eve were innocents who walked with God and served His will in serene peace and plenty. There would be no end to this holy relationship unless they ate of the tree of the knowledge of good and evil.

Neither Adam nor Eve shaped a rebellious thought in their innocence. It was satan who was cast down from Heaven in his failed rebellion that tempted Eve with these words, "⁵ For God knows that on the day you eat from it your eyes will be opened, and you will become like God, knowing good and evil" (Genesis 3:5).

Mankind has never stopped pursuing knowledge. From the praise given to the smartest student in the class to the latest developments in our sciences of every discipline, we are locked in a race to be smarter, better, and more powerful. We excel at developing new instruments of war or risk annihilation.

Medical researchers have done wonders as they conquer one disease after another. They have developed procedures to fix broken bones and organs while relieving pain and restoring function. We live much longer than the average life expectancy when Jesus dwelled among us. But in the end, we all die. "[36] For what shall it profit a man, if he shall gain the whole world, and lose his own soul?" (Mark 8:36). Our wisdom is briefly focused on this physical world we have drenched in our sin as we follow satan's relentless manipulation. How foolish is that? Jesus Christ lived, died, rose from death, and ascended back to His Father's side. He will never die again. He did it for you, me, and everyone who believes in Him and repents of our sins. "[25] Jesus said to her, 'I am the resurrection and the life. The one who believes in me will live, even though they die; [26] and whoever lives by believing in me will never die. Do you believe this?'" (John 11:25–26).

Salvation comes when we lift our eyes up to the heavenly kingdom of Jesus Christ by focusing them on the Holy Bible. Jesus is most certainly "the Gift that keeps on giving!"

Thanks be to God that we share Jesus Christ's blood-shed gift of grace!

God Is Our Refuge

Our perspective on the distance between God and ourselves is indeed our perspective.

When we are feeling secure and satisfied, many give little or no thought of Jesus Christ because we credit ourselves for this condition. This is the philosophy of works. This philosophy holds that every good thing rests upon generations of human accomplishments in every physical art or industry. We have the best medicine, the best industries, and the best defenses made by mankind.

What of our perspective when a handful of terrorists use box cutters and suicidal devotion to their religion to bring down destruction and death to thousands of Americans? We flood back to our churches and lift prayers to God in the sacred name of Jesus Christ, our risen Lord and Savior.

Sadly, in short order, our churches emptied of the overflowing congregations. As we regained our personal composure and stepped away from the box in which we keep Jesus, our churches.

Consider recent events and the gathering darkness of evil storms rising across the globe. Some will question where God resides and how He can let this happen. Many of our Christian churches will see rising attendance as we pray for our families and friends who are most directly in harm's way. We will also pray for peace as we hear sermons devoted to it.

God is always with us. God is our refuge and strength, "A very ready help in trouble" (Psalm 46:1). He is at our side in Jesus Christ wherever and whenever we find ourselves. When we believe and accept Jesus as our risen Lord and Savior, He dwells within our hearts through the Holy Spirit.

Jesus descended from His heavenly kingdom to join us in our flesh. Jesus created the New Testament in His shed blood on the cross. He is always with us. We must study His Word and worship Him so that we may believe in Him and be saved as we repent of our sins in His holy name. Jesus told Pilate that His kingdom is not of this world (John 18:36).

Jesus tells us,

> [1] Let not your heart be troubled: ye believe in God, believe also in me. [2] In my Father's house are many mansions: if it were not so, I would have told you. I go to prepare a place for you. [3] And if I go and prepare a place for you, I will come again, and receive you unto myself; that where I am, there ye may be also. (John 14:1–3)

Let us pray that our thoughts, words, and deeds are God's will for each of us. May we serve His will, "[7] and the peace of God, which surpasses all understanding, will guard your hearts and minds through Christ Jesus" (Philippians 4:7). May we open our hearts to Him and pass through the doors of His church every Sunday.

God of All People

Today's devotion focuses on Cyrus, whom God's prophet Isaiah identified as God's anointed one. This is a status reserved for people specifically chosen by God to perform on His behalf, like kings or priests of Israel.

Cyrus is special because he was not a Jew and didn't know our God, much less believe in Him. This is what the Lord says to Cyrus, His anointed, "Whom I have taken by the right hand, To subdue nations before him And to undo the weapons belt on the waist of kings; To open doors before him so that gates will not be shut" (Isaiah 45).

Cyrus conquered most of the known world under God's protection and direction without knowing God. Cyrus was not aware that he was freeing God's people from slavery and lives exiled from the promised land God had given them. The restoration of Israel in the promised land would set the stage for them to rebuild the temple that Jesus Christ would visit as a child and later as an adult in His Messianic mission to provide the way home to Heaven where we become children of God, forever.

> [25] Jesus said to her, "I am the resurrection and the life. The one who believes in me will live, even though they die; [26] and whoever lives by believing in me will never die. Do you believe this?" (John 11:25–26)

As we live lives of decades focused upon ourselves and the broken world around us, He sees every moment in time eternal. Through Jesus's shed blood and prayer for us from the cross: "[34] Then Jesus said, 'Father, forgive them, for they do not know what they do'" (Luke 23:34). Even as nonbelievers perform acts and shout words that are horrific to Christians and Jews, we must remain faithful in Jesus Christ.

In Him, we must know that even their most evil and heinous acts cannot defeat Him or block His way for us to become children of God in Heaven forever. The peace He offers us is linked inextricably to our faith in Him. "⁷ And the peace of God, which surpasses all understanding, will guard your hearts and minds through Christ Jesus" (Philippians 4:7).

May we lift prayers for the people of Israel and everyone who defends them in these days of death and horror. Let us pray for everyone who is slain, threatened, or harmed by Hamas and their allies, that they may be delivered from this evil in victory over these enemies. Let us pray that everyone who dies at their hands may be delivered into Heaven.

Thanks be to God in every circumstance in the sure and certain hope that Jesus Christ gives us through His shed blood and promise of eternal life in Him. This too shall pass. If we pass before Christ's return, know we are with Him. I thank Him that we share our love in Him here and now.

His Chosen People

Abraham is the patriarch of Israel, the Jewish people. God spoke this promise as the original covenant between Himself and Abraham:

> "² I will make you into a great nation, and I will bless you; I will make your name great, and you will be a blessing. ³ I will bless those who bless you, and whoever curses you I will curse; and all peoples on earth will be blessed through you." (Genesis 12:2–3)

The Old Testament of the Holy Bible is founded upon this covenant between God and Israel. He set His chosen people apart from the rest of humanity as His vine winding through human history that would bear holy fruit, "all peoples on earth will be blessed through you."

But Israel would not honor God's Word. As we read the Old Testament, it is an unending cycle of Israel disregarding God's commandments and trampling upon His blessings to them. They worshiped pagan idols, intermarried with other peoples while ignoring God, even killing His prophets who preached His Word to them. Time and again, they would fall into ruin and live in despair. They would then turn back to God in prayer and repentance. He would restore them because He never forgets His promises. Then, the descent into sin and away from Him would begin again. This is the garden of Eden replayed over and over again.

Jesus Christ, God's only Son, was born a Jew in the line of King David as predicted by God's prophets. It is through Him that "all peoples on earth will be blessed through you." Jesus lived in our flesh without any sin at all. "[16] For God so loved the world that he gave his one and only Son, that whoever believes in him shall not perish but have eternal life" (John 3:16).

The New Testament is written in Jesus Christ's shed blood from the Cross for "whoever believes in him." The Apostle Paul wrote to the congregations at Galatia, "[28] There is neither Jew nor Gentile, neither slave nor free, nor is there male and female, for you are all one in Christ Jesus" (Galatians 3:28). Jesus Christ's blood-shed grace is not constrained by any convention of human nature or culture or biology. As Jesus told Pontius Pilate as Pilate tried Jesus on the false charges brought against Him: "[36] Jesus answered, My kingdom is not of this world: if my kingdom were of this world, then would my servants fight, that I should not be delivered to the Jews: but now is my kingdom not from hence" (John 18:36).

Jesus died for each one of us personally. He welcomes our repentant spirit that believes in Him to Himself when our flesh fails. "[7] and the peace of God, which surpasses all understanding, will guard your hearts and minds through Christ Jesus" (Philippians 4:7).

Our journey in this corrupted flesh is brief and sometimes difficult. May we open our hearts to His saving grace in every circumstance.

SELECTED DEVOTIONS

His Peace or Mine?

The *Merriam-Webster* definition for "peace" is "a state of tranquility or quiet: such as freedom from civil disturbance."

> [Jesus said] "When the Son of Man comes in His glory…He will separate people one from another as a shepherd separates the sheep from the goats. Then the King will say to those on His right, 'Come, you who are blessed by My Father, inherit the Kingdom prepared for you from the foundation of the world. For I was hungry and you gave Me food, I was thirsty and you gave Me drink, I was a stranger and you welcomed Me, I was naked and you clothed Me, I was sick and you visited Me, I was in prison and you came to Me.' Then the righteous will answer Him, saying, 'Lord, when did we see You hungry and feed You, or thirsty and give You drink? And when did we see You a stranger and welcome You, or naked and clothe You? And when did we see You sick or in prison and visit You?' And the King will answer them, 'Truly, I say to you, as you did it to one of the least of these My brothers, you did it to Me.' Then He will say to those on His left, 'Depart from Me, you cursed, into the eternal fire prepared for the devil and his angels. For I was hungry and you gave Me no food, I was thirsty and you gave Me no drink Truly, I say to you, as you did not do it to one of the least of these, you did not do it to Me.'" (Matthew 25:31a, 32b, 34–42, 45b–46)

Christians were puzzled. They did not recall seeing Him hungry, thirsty, naked, sick, or in prison. They told Him so. Those who

He condemned to eternal fire alongside satan were as confused and desperate in their denials.

The saved and the damned shared one thing in common. They had peace of mind. The peace of mind for the damned is founded on satisfying themselves through self-indulgence and personal pleasure without regard for the love and lessons Jesus Christ offers us. They knew not Jesus, or worse, they denied Him.

The peace of Christians rest on this:

> [4] Rejoice in the Lord always. Again I will say, rejoice! [5] Let your gentleness be known to all men. The Lord is at hand. [6] Be anxious for nothing, but in everything by prayer and supplication, with thanksgiving, let your requests be made known to God; [7] and the peace of God, which surpasses all understanding, will guard your hearts and minds through Christ Jesus. (Philippians 4:4–7)

Both groups did what was natural. For born-again Christians, natural is forever changed when we accept Jesus Christ. We repent of our sins and see everything through Him. While sinners still, our faith in Christ changes our relationship with our fellow man too. Jesus is with us always.

Home Is Where the Heart Is

> "Lord, You have been our dwelling place in all generations. Before the mountains were brought forth, or ever You had formed the earth and the world, from everlasting to everlasting You are God." (Psalm 90:1–2)

We are spiritual beings outside of time and space who are sojourning here in this temporal flesh for a brief moment in time. As Jesus told Pontius Pilate, "My kingdom is not of this world. If My kingdom were of this world, My servants would be fighting so that I would not be handed over to the Jews; but as it is, My kingdom is not of this realm" (John 18:36).

When we read the Word of God in the Holy Bible, we are being educated in the one Truth that is eternal. Jesus Christ was present, as God brought forth His creation into this physical realm.

> For by him were all things created, that are in heaven, and that are in earth, visible and invisible, whether they be thrones, or dominions, or principalities, or powers: all things were created by him, and for him. (Colossians 1:16)

When we open our hearts to Jesus, He extends our consciousness to the Father, the Son, and the Holy Spirit.

> If you love me, keep my commands. And I will ask the Father, and he will give you another advocate to help you and be with you forever—the Spirit of truth. The world cannot accept him, because it neither sees him nor knows him. But you know him, for he lives with you and will be in you. (John 14:15–17)

When we Christians breathe our last, we do not die. We do, indeed, go home to join all the Christians who have gone ahead of us to be at home in Jesus Christ forever. One day, we will all be home for Christmas celebrating forever in His peace and love for us. He frees from this speck of corrupted dust forever.

> [14] Let not your heart be troubled: ye believe in God, believe also in me. [2] In my Father's house are many mansions: if it were not so, I would have told you. I go to prepare a place for you. [3] And if I go and prepare a place for you, I will

come again, and receive you unto myself; that where I am, there ye may be also. (John 14:1–3)

I thank God we have given our hearts to Jesus to become sons and daughters of God in Heaven.

Godforsaken?

"Godforsaken" is a term we don't hear every day. Thanks be to God. I recall it as a line in some science fiction movie where it was used for dramatic affect.

It led me to consider God's presence throughout the entire universe. Astrophysicists are fond of reminding us of the incomprehensible dimensions of creation where distance is measured by the distance light travels in a year (the speed of light is 186,000 miles per second). The farthest observable star with current technology is five billion light-years from earth. I don't want to do the math to miles.

God is present in every part of His creation.

> Where shall I go from Your Spirit? Or where shall I flee from Your presence? If I ascend to heaven, You are there! If I make my bed in Sheol, You are there! If I take the wings of the morning and dwell in the uttermost parts of the sea, even there Your hand shall lead me, and Your right hand shall hold me. (Psalm 139:7–10)

Here, the psalmist is not trying to flee God. No, he is describing the unfathomable divine nature of our heavenly Father. There is no place we can go to leave God behind.

The human imagination is incapable of defining His infinite nature outside the confines of our physical world. I believe this is particularly difficult for minds that focus intently on the physical in order to define it, understand how it works, and what makes it all tick. Many scientists (but not all) are atheists. Their minds are trapped in a construct limited by their inability to comprehend God who is unbound by their rules and theories developed across generations of study.

We know of only one instance where "Godforsaken" actually applied. Jesus hung on the cross suffering and dying as He accepted every sin ever committed by everyone from Adam to the last sinner before Christ returns in judgment. God's perfectly innocent Son became soiled beyond our comprehension with the load of all that sin. "[46] And about the ninth hour Jesus cried with a loud voice, saying, Eli, Eli, lama sabachthani? that is to say, My God, my God, why hast thou forsaken me?" (Matthew 27:46).

"[23] For the wages of sin is death" (Romans 6:23). God does not abide sin. Jesus chose to take all our sins upon Himself and was separated from His Father for us. Christ used death as the way to confront and defeat satan, sin, and death forever, for everyone who believes in Him and repents of our sins.

On Easter Sunday, God raised Jesus from death forever, so He could rejoin His Father in Heaven. Jesus tells us, "[2] I go to prepare a place for you. [3] And if I go and prepare a place for you, I will come again, and receive you unto myself; that where I am, there ye may be also" (John 14:2–3).

Thanks be to God!

How Close to Jesus?

We file into our churches on Sundays to gather around Jesus Christ. We drink His blood and eat His flesh in Holy Communion. Our hearts and minds are focused on our Him for an hour, perhaps two or three with Bible study and fellowship. We are celebrating our faith in Jesus among fellow Christians openly and confidently. We are close to Him.

At the end of services, we file back out, maybe pausing to shake our pastor's hand and exchange a word before crossing the threshold to exit into the rest of our lives. How close are we to Jesus for the 165 hours before we return for services next week?

Well, it depends, doesn't it? Let us consider Peter of whom Jesus said, "¹⁸ And I tell you that you are Peter, and on this rock I will build my church, and the gates of Hades will not overcome it" (Matthew 16:18).

Jesus knew how Peter would behave on the night Jesus was betrayed and delivered to the Jews. Peter would fall asleep after Jesus asked him to be with Him as He prayed in the garden of Gethsemane. Peter fled with the other disciples to avoid being identified as Jesus's apostles and arrested. Peter followed Jesus now in custody, from a distance to observe while avoiding arrest.

Jesus warned His disciples that they would all abandon Him when He was betrayed. Peter replied to this warning with these words:

> ²⁹ Peter said to him, "Even if everyone else deserts you, I never will." ³⁰ Jesus replied, "I tell you the truth, Peter—this very night, before the rooster crows twice, you will deny three times that you even know me." ³¹ "No!" Peter declared emphatically. "Even if I have to die with you, I will never deny you!" And all the others vowed the same. (Mark 14:29–31)

> The night played out just as Jesus had predicted. Peter was challenged by others who recognized him as Jesus's disciple. On the third accusation he replied, ⁶⁰ But Peter said, "Man, I do not know what you are saying!" Immediately, while he was still speaking, the rooster crowed. ⁶¹ And the Lord turned and looked at Peter. Then Peter remembered the word of the Lord, how He had said to him, "Before the rooster crows, you will deny Me three times." ⁶² So Peter went out and wept bitterly. (Luke 22:60–62)

I know that I feel hesitant to share my faith in Jesus sometimes. But my silence is what satan wants and I am ashamed. I pray for forgiveness and the strength to walk beside Jesus openly while sharing Him with everyone I may. That is what Jesus wants.

May we thank Jesus for His unending grace for us as we fail again and again. May we pray for the strength and confidence of faith to share You in every circumstance. Thy will be done Jesus, not mine.

Jealousy

The Word of God, our Holy Bible, is a long and glorious scroll of the history of God's relationship with us, whom He created. It is not crafted to ensure that everything is recorded in the best possible light. Its heroes and heroines are presented with all of the sins and shortcomings that are us.

It begins with Adam and Eve who regularly walk with God in the garden and hear Him speak directly to them within a perfect setting. This loving relationship is shattered when they listen to satan and violate the single commandment God gave them. Under the influence of satan, they substitute their judgment for God's and become convinced God is afraid that they will become like Him.

Jealousy is at the root of satan's strategy to separate us from God and condemn us to share eternal damnation with satan. The noble declaration that "All men are created equal" is too easily corrupted.

The Truth is:

> [9] Well then, should we conclude that we Jews are better than others? No, not at all, for we have already shown that all people, whether Jews or Gentiles are under the power of sin. [19] Obviously, the law applies to those to whom it was given, for its purpose is to keep people from having excuses, and to show that the entire world is guilty before God. [20] For no one can ever be made right with God by doing what the law commands. The law simply shows us how sinful we are. (Romans 3:9, 19–20).

> [9] To some who were confident of their own righteousness and looked down on everyone else, Jesus told this parable: [10] "Two men went up to the temple to pray, one a Pharisee and the other a tax collector. [11] The Pharisee stood by himself and prayed: 'God, I thank you that I am not like other people—robbers, evildoers, adulterers—or even like this tax collector. [12] I fast twice a week and give a tenth of all I get.' [13] "But the tax collector stood at a distance. He would not even look up to heaven, but beat his breast and said, 'God, have mercy on me, a sinner.' [14] "I tell you that this man, rather than the other, went home justified before God. For all those who exalt themselves will be humbled, and those who humble themselves will be exalted." (Luke 18:9–14)

The moment we shift our gaze down from Jesus Christ to one another for comparison, we are devoting ourselves to satan. May we prostrate ourselves at the foot of the cross humbly pleading for the undeserved grace that bleeds from Jesus's side. Let us not look around at others there to take pride in ourselves. Then, we look away from Christ's grace and step toward satan.

> [6] Jesus saith unto him, I am the way, the truth, and the life: no man cometh unto the Father, but by me. (John 14:6)

How Evil Are We?

How evil are we? It is up to us. God creates each one of us with our own free will. Truly, we decide who we are. We are quick to claim, "I have rights!" when something or someone restrains us from doing what we want. When caught and facing prosecution, we hear, "It's not my fault!"

Ask any police officer about the people they see every day. They quickly come to realize that free will is at the core of crime, as some among us choose to use violence or deception to take from others what they desire.

There is a spectrum of evil among all of us. Most of us are petty criminals/sinners. Most of us realize the error of our ways and restrain ourselves to some degree. We also struggle to justify what we have done with false rationalizations like "They deserved it!" or "I asked, but they were selfish and denied me what I deserve!" There are those who rush in to excuse our criminal/sinful behavior because our circumstances aren't right.

There is a small fraction of us who aren't concerned about justification. Sometimes, we encounter those who do heinous things simply because it gives them pleasure. The secular term is "sociopath." They do not bother with any pretense of justification.

God is unchanging. He presents us with the Law in the Old Testament. It clearly defines sin. There is one penalty for any sin of any kind. It is death, which began with Adam and Eve when they listened to satan and defied God. Satan is the original cheerleader for sin and convinced them that what they did was justified.

God does not restrain our free will as we live out our lives in our flesh. We are free to do whatever wish, but the consequence is unwavering. God's love for us is also beyond our comprehension and unwavering.

"[16] For God so loved the world, that He gave His only begotten Son, that whoever believes in Him shall not perish, but have eternal life" (John 3:16). "[6] Jesus answered, 'I am the way and the truth and the life. No one comes to the Father except through me'" (John 14:6). At Matthew 4:16, Jesus tells us, "[17] From that time Jesus began to preach and to say, Repent, for the Kingdom of Heaven is at hand."

Only when we believe Jesus is our risen Lord and Savior and confess our sins with repentance are we saved. It is our personal choice; no one can make it for us. No one else may excuse us. Look not to justify yourself or to listen to others justify you. If you do this, you die. God knows who we choose to be in our hearts.

May we share Jesus with everyone so they may repent and be saved by His blood-shed grace forever.

Humbly Before God

How we see ourselves is perhaps our greatest stumbling block in our path along the way that Jesus Christ gave His life to provide us. The original sin in which we dwell steeps us into pride.

Pride is the path satan used to change the hearts of Eve, then Adam. A friend pointed out that ego upsets many of us as we struggle to learn the right relationship with our Creator. We are His, He is not ours. His will be done, not ours. He authors the commandments and sets the laws for us to obey before us. Satan couldn't abide this because his ego convinces him that he is superior to God. "EGO" stands for Easing God Out.

I know I still have that problem after a lifetime of the Holy Spirit dwelling within me. The Holy Spirit has wrought wonderful changes in my spirit and educates me every day. I am grateful to God for His patience with my ego. I don't believe my ego is as large as it used to be. But it distracts me still from God's Word, will, and His Son's saving grace.

It is my prayer that I never challenge Him or doubt His will and Word. Let us learn to accept them particularly when we can't understand it as we read it. May we faithfully accept every word in grateful submission to His perfection. Further, God, help us not to fill in the blanks to suit ourselves. May we accept that we cannot know the mind of God.

> [10] But God has revealed them to us through His Spirit. For the Spirit searches all things, yes, the deep things of God. [11] For what man knows the things of a man except the spirit of the man

> which is in him? Even so no one knows the things of God except the Spirit of God. [12] Now we have received, not the spirit of the world, but the Spirit who is from God, that we might know the things that have been freely given to us by God. (1 Corinthians 2:10–12)

Peter presumed to tell Jesus that Jesus could never submit to death in Jerusalem, when Jesus told His disciples that this must happen. "[23] Jesus turned and said to Peter, 'Get behind me, satan! You are a stumbling block to me; you do not have in mind the concerns of God, but merely human concerns'" (Matthew 16:23).

May we pray to seek complete submission to God. "[4] Therefore, whoever takes the lowly position of this child is the greatest in the kingdom of heaven. [5] And whoever welcomes one such child in my name welcomes me" (Matthew 18:4–5).

May we pray to be children of God who don't muddy our clothes washed clean in Christ's own blood.

Live Free or Die

"Live Free or Die" is the state motto of New Hampshire. It is credited to General John Stark, the state's preeminent Revolutionary War hero.

This sentiment was crafted within the circumstances of violence that is horribly unique to warfare. War is where death becomes a common acquaintance in its most grotesque and frightening forms. It is where heroes give their lives for their country and their brothers-in-arms freely. They placed themselves in harm's way to oust the oppressors and establish a nation founded on freedom and justice for all.

Our founders' Declaration of Independence and all that followed to defeat the most powerful army, navy, and nation on earth was voluntary.

This sentiment was not born in our revolutionary spirit. It is found throughout the Word of God who created us with unfettered free will. God has never been nor will He ever be our oppressor. He is our heavenly Father. "¹⁶ For God so loved the world, that he gave his only begotten Son, that whosoever believeth in him should not perish, but have everlasting life" (John 3:16).

Jesus Christ explained the path to true freedom to those who believed in Him. "³¹ Then said Jesus to those Jews which believed on him, If ye continue in my word, then are ye my disciples indeed; ³² and ye shall know the truth, and the truth shall make you free" (John 8:31–32).

Jesus was born to wage war against satan, sin, and death for you, me, and every man, woman, or child ever born. He was born into our flesh to fight for us, alongside us, in our flesh. Jesus confronted satan and his minions in our flesh and defeated them. He suffered most horribly on the cross as He took every sin ever committed upon Himself while praying. "³⁴ Then Jesus said, Father, forgive them, for they do not know what they do" (Luke 23:34).

In death, Jesus descended into hell where He defeated satan, sin, sin, and death forever before rising victorious on the third day to share His victory with us. Before He ascended back into Heaven from whence He came, He shared these words with us, "¹⁴ Let not your heart be troubled: ye believe in God, believe also in me. ² In my Father's house are many mansions: if it were not so, I would have told you. I go to prepare a place for you. ³ And if I go and prepare a place for you, I will come again, and receive you unto myself; that where I am, there ye may be also" (John 14:1–3).

Born again in Christ, we live free and never die! Lift up the Bible and study the Word to arm yourself in Him for eternal victory.

I Believe in Jesus

What does Jesus mean when He says, "¹⁶ He who believes and is baptized will be saved; but he who does not believe will be condemned" (Mark 16:16).

Satan and his minions believe in Jesus Christ, the only begotten Son of God. They never fared well in their confrontations with Him. They refuse to accept His blood-shed gift of grace. They continue to fight against God. They never repent of the sins they enjoy and embrace. They celebrate them.

It is our human nature to rationalize and blur the lines to support our personal beliefs, situations, and practices. At least satan is clear and evidently convincing when he continues to be the very definition of sinful evil while refusing to repent or acknowledge the superiority of God.

The Nicene Creed is shared by millions of Christians worldwide. It defines our belief in God the Father, Jesus Christ, and the Holy Spirit. Here is what it says about Jesus,

> I believe in one Lord Jesus Christ, the Only Begotten Son of God, born of the Father before all ages. God from God, Light from Light, true God from true God, begotten, not made, being of one substance with the Father; through him all things were made. For us men and for our salvation he came down from heaven, and by the Holy Spirit was incarnate of the Virgin Mary and became man. For our sake he was crucified under Pontius Pilate, he suffered death and was buried, and rose again on the third day in accordance with the Scriptures. He ascended into heaven and is seated at the right hand of the Father. He will come again in glory to judge the living and the dead and his kingdom will have no end.

Our faith in Jesus Christ defines our relationship with Him. Jesus preached these words after enduring forty days of temptation in the desert. "[15] And saying, The time is fulfilled, and the kingdom of God is at hand: repent ye, and believe the gospel" (Mark 1:15). Jesus also shared these words with us: "[6] Jesus saith unto him, I am the way, the truth, and the life: no man cometh unto the Father, but by me" (John 14:6).

We must believe, submit, and repent of our sins in the holy name of Jesus Christ. He is our risen Lord and Savior! Thanks be to God! Do you believe?

Thanks be to God that we share our faith in Jesus Christ, which never fails us.

Ignorant Hostages

> And suddenly there was with the angel a multitude of the heavenly host praising God and saying, "Glory to God in the highest, and on earth peace among those with whom He is pleased!" (Luke 2:13–14)

The events surrounding the angelic announcement of the Jesus's birth is spectacular. The darkness of night is banished by heavenly light as the first angel appears to speak to the shepherds below in the field. Suddenly, he is joined by a multitude of angels singing the praises of Jesus and sharing the most wonderful news of His mission among us in our flesh.

I must admit that I have wondered why they are so happy and joyful at our salvation. After all, each of us are descendants of Adam and Eve who chose to abandon God, our Creator, and follow satan's words. One cannot begin to count the number of sins we have committed over the time since they left Eden. We turn our backs to God.

Then I recall the parable Jesus told of the lost son, who took his inheritance and abandoned his father to squander it and himself on wild living. His father welcomed him back when he returned starving and filthy seeking a job. But his father knew him and loved him.

More recently, I watched the joyful welcomes celebrated when some of the hostages Hamas violently took from Israel on October 7, 2023. They were in the darkness of tunnels and the deeper darkness of depravity from their captors. The joyful light and love from their families, loved ones, and strangers upon their return fills the heart with gratitude upon their salvation from that captivity.

We all share our Creator, our Savior, and the Holy Spirit. We are born ignorant of Him into a dark world of corrupted flesh. We are held captive in satan's kingdom on earth, in a darkness far deeper than those tunnels Hamas constructed. Our heavenly Father and His angels know this and see us struggling in this trap of our own design without hope. Then

> [16] For God so loved the world that he gave his one and only Son, that whoever believes in him shall not perish but have eternal life. [17] For God did not send his Son into the world to condemn the world, but to save the world through him. (John 3:16–17)

> [8] For it is by grace you have been saved, through faith—and this is not from yourselves, it is the gift of God—[9] not by works, so that no one can boast. (Ephesians 2:8–9)

> [17] So faith comes from hearing, and hearing by the word of Christ. (Romans 10:17)

The heavenly hosts knew that Jesus Christ is the Word made flesh. He is the ransom that frees all who believe in Him from the bondage of sin in satan forever. Of course, they are celebrating His birth among us with great joy. We are coming home through Him and Him alone. Merry Christmas forever!

Sincerest Flattery

The Old Testament is the Law. That is the Ten Commandments that God delivered to Moses carved into stone. The penalty for failure to obey them is death.

God delegated authority to Moses and His priests to elaborate on the commandments. They crafted a detailed collection of laws and the sacrifices to be offered for forgiveness and to avoid the penalty of death in the book of Leviticus.

No one ever came close to living a life free of sin. Yet quickly, we began to compare ourselves with others to assure ourselves that we were more pure and closer to God. Consider the parable of the tax collector and Pharisee,

> ⁹ Now He also told this parable to some people who trusted in themselves that they were righteous, and viewed others with contempt: ¹⁰ "Two men went up into the temple to pray, one a Pharisee and the other a tax collector. ¹¹ The Pharisee stood and began praying this in regard to himself: 'God, I thank You that I am not like other people: swindlers, crooked, adulterers, or even like this tax collector. ¹² I fast twice a week; I pay tithes of all that I get.' ¹³ But the tax collector, standing some distance away, was even unwilling to raise his eyes toward heaven, but was beating his chest, saying, 'God, be merciful to me, the sinner!' ¹⁴ I tell you, this man went to his house justified rather than the other one; for everyone who exalts himself will be humbled, but the one who humbles himself will be exalted." (Luke 18:9–14)

The Apostle Paul wrote to the church of the Thessalonians, praising them,

> ⁶ You became imitators of us and of the Lord, for you welcomed the message in the midst of severe suffering with the joy given by the Holy Spirit. ⁷ And so you became a model to all the believers in Macedonia and Achaia. ⁸ The Lord's message rang out from you not only in Macedonia and Achaia—your faith in God has become known everywhere. (1 Thessalonians: 6–8)

Paul praises them for becoming "imitators of us and of the Lord." As Paul and his fellow apostles strove imperfectly to live as examples for our Lord, so did the Christians of Thessalonica. Let us pray to be His examples that draw people to Him. It is important that we share that we don't deserve His grace either. "⁸ For it is by grace you have been saved, through faith—and this is not from yourselves, it is the gift of God—⁹ not by works, so that no one can boast" (Ephesians 2:8–9).

Jesus Christ is the final, perfect sacrifice for every sin. We fail to imitate our risen Lord and Savior perfectly and always need His blood-shed grace. His grace never fails for those who believe in Him and repent. Thanks be to God!

It is our shared love in Jesus that delivers us to eternally into His holy family.

Come and See

Have you ever been convinced of the performance of a product or service by the commercials that come at you from every direction? Does the carefully selected spokesperson speaking meticulously arranged words make you a true believer of whatever it is they are trying to sell you?

While young and impressionable without much experience to weigh the truth or reliability of the story, perhaps we were. But experience and disappointment sharpen our judgment in ways we probably wish they hadn't.

This principle is particularly true in judging people you meet from the casual to the most intimate. The pain resulting from lies or failure to keep promises made to you may make you grow up too quickly and hobble your future relationships. Past betrayals shape future judgments of people we don't know and may not trust through no fault of their own.

All of this comes to bear when we share Jesus Christ with others. Their personal experiences with others, the stories related to them commercially or one on one, set the stage upon which we present the gospel to them.

> ⁴³ The next day He decided to go to Galilee, and He found Philip. And Jesus said to him,

"Follow Me." ⁴⁴ Now Philip was from Bethsaida, the city of Andrew and Peter. ⁴⁵ Philip found Nathanael and said to him, "We have found Him of whom Moses wrote in the Law, and the prophets also wrote: Jesus the son of Joseph, from Nazareth!" ⁴⁶ Nathanael said to him, "Can anything good be from Nazareth?" Philip said to him, "Come and see." (John 1:43–46)

Philip was clearly a true believer in Jesus Christ. He was excited about knowing the Messiah personally and rushed to share this Good News with Nathanael, so he too would come to Christ. Nathanael reacted to this news in much the same way you or I would have probably done. Philip is not Jesus.

All Jesus had to say to Philip was "Follow Me." Philip knew what he felt and what he had come to know about Jesus from meeting Him and hearing His divine invitation to join Him. Philip didn't wish to waste time debating the authenticity of Jesus Christ with Nathanael. So he simply invited Nathanael to "Come and see."

We can't bring our family, loved ones, friends, or strangers to meet Jesus face-to-face. But we can invite them to join us in Bible study and church services. "¹⁷ So faith comes from hearing, and hearing by the word of Christ" (Romans 10:17).

Our relationship with our risen Lord and Savior, Jesus Christ is the most intimate relationship we can experience because He is God. "¹⁶ For God so loved the world, that He gave His only begotten Son, that whoever believes in Him shall not perish, but have eternal life" (John 3:16).

Let us invite everyone to "Come and see." I pray they come to believe and are saved in Jesus Christ forever.

Immanuel

"¹⁴ Therefore the Lord Himself will give you a sign: Behold, the virgin shall conceive and bear a Son, and shall call His name Immanuel" (Isaiah 7:14). Isaiah was perhaps the most prolific and specific Old Testament prophet. The words above are words of God spoken to him thousands of years before Jesus was born into our flesh from the Virgin Mary's womb.

In the Christmas season, we celebrate the birth of Jesus Christ, our risen Lord and Savior. He would live to die for us and then after descending into hell to defeat satan, sin, and death forever, He would rise on the third day. (But that part of the gospel is for Easter.)

The words from God that Isaiah recorded so many years before Jesus's birth include "and shall call His name Immanuel." Immanuel is a Hebrew name which means "God with us."

The hymn "O Come O Come Emmanuel" was originally sung by monks in medieval times as worship. Songs of worship provided a beautiful way of memorizing worship before the printing press provided a way of mass-producing texts. Even then, most people couldn't read. This hymn was translated in the 1800s and the tune we sing was crafted to fit the text. It is now our privilege to join the ancient Christian monks who gave voice to it centuries ago.

This hymn is a beautiful masterpiece that warms our hearts as we give voice to its words that come from God. I believe the Holy Spirit that lives within us provides the warmth and peace that envelopes us during this most holy time of year. May we share Immanuel with those who don't yet know Him so they may be saved in His blood-shed grace. "[7] And the peace of God, which surpasses all understanding, will guard your hearts and minds through Christ Jesus" (Philippians 4:7).

God is indeed always with us all we have to do is "Open Up Your Heart and Let the Sun Son Shine In" (McGuire Sisters 1955 with one great change).

Merry Christmas!

Never Tire of the Word

Have you ever heard someone comment on the "same old sermon" Sunday after Sunday? Or more likely, "The church has to wake up and join the modern world"?

We even hear these calls for modernization of the Christian church from some of our most prominent leaders. This tension with the boredom or disappointment with the unchanging Word of God has become a source of increasing criticism of the church. It goes beyond debate to hostility toward the Word of God for being "backward," "racist," "sexist," or just plain "bigoted."

People of faith who truly accept Jesus Christ as our risen Lord and Savior, the only begotten Son of God, do not tire of the Word or insist on God making concessions to our personal tastes or opinions.

God does not negotiate with us so that we may become His children. Jesus Christ did not suffer and die under the weight of some of our sins. Jesus didn't pick or choose who may be eligible for salvation from His shed blood. Nor did Jesus rise from death on the third day with a list of whom He would forgive based upon their sins. God's unchanging Word is founded on His love for all of us.

> "[16] For God so loved the world, that He gave His only Son, so that everyone who believes in Him will not perish, but have eternal life." (John 3:16)

As we study His Word, we begin to journey along the way Jesus Christ fashioned for us in His shed blood. "[17] So then faith comes by hearing, and hearing by the Word of God" (Romans 10:17).

It is the Word of God that strengthens us as sin and satan, wage an unrelenting attack against our faith and the salvation that is available only through Jesus Christ. "[6] Jesus answered, 'I am the way and the truth and the life. No one comes to the Father except through me'" (John 14:6).

We have no place to change the one and only way back to God. It is His construction, paved with the blood of His only begotten Son, Jesus Christ.

When we read His Word in Bible study, we hear something new and learn something holy we did not understand before.

May we never tire of the Word and may we continue to study the Word, finding it new with every reading. Please attend the church of your choice every Sunday and be reinvigorated in Him through His Word.

In Weakness

Therefore, in order to keep me from becoming conceited, I was given a thorn in my flesh, a messenger of satan, to torment me.

> [8] Three times I pleaded with the Lord to take it away from me. [9] But he said to me, "My grace is sufficient for you, for my power is made perfect in weakness." Therefore I will boast all the more gladly about my weaknesses, so that Christ's power may rest on me. [10] That is why, for Christ's sake, I delight in weaknesses, in insults, in hardships, in persecutions, in difficulties. For when I am weak, then I am strong. (2 Corinthians 7–10)

This is Paul testifying to the congregation at Corinth about himself as an apostle of God. The Corinthians were in turmoil as different factions chose different interpretations of what the Word of God meant. There were many who had never repented of their sins in Jesus's name. Today, we see many different interpretations of the gospels leading to many different Christian churches.

Paul was using himself to explain a righteous relationship with God through Jesus Christ. It is one of submission and devotion to the Word of God made flesh, Jesus Christ. The moment we assume that we may pick or choose what part of the Bible is real and what is not, we are placing ourselves in a superior position to God.

We cannot submit to God in Jesus Christ as we refuse to accept His Word as perfect and unchanging.

Jesus tells us, "[6] Jesus saith unto him, I am the way, the truth, and the life: no man cometh unto the Father, but by me" (John 14:6).

Paul wrote to the Corinthians, "Therefore I will boast all the more gladly about my weaknesses, so that Christ's power may rest on me. Let us pray daily to God in Jesus's name that we may submit to God's every Word He has delivered to us in the Holy Bible." The Old Testament comes to us through His prophets and others appointed by God to hold the pen for His direction. The New Testament is written in the blood of Jesus Christ who prayed these words on the night in which He was betrayed, "³⁹ And He went a little farther, and fell on His face and prayed, saying, 'O My Father, if it be possible, let this cup pass from Me; nevertheless, not as I will, but as Thou wilt'" (Matthew 26:39).

May we always pray that our hearts are open to the Holy Spirit and that we understand His words for us as holy instruction. May we accept those words submissively. Pray that our words to others are His, not ours so that we reflect Jesus Christ clearly without corrupting His words with our thoughts. Thank you, Jesus!

Internal Conflict

The conflict that surrounds us never ends, many of us are becoming convinced that we are living in the end-times.

The end-times herald the return of Jesus Christ to us. Within our Christian denominations and congregations conflict rises over the end-times. Some simply dismiss them as meaningless rhetoric contained in the pages of the Holy Bible that are merely allegorical. Another explanation which discounts these passages say that errors were made over the centuries in the translation of the biblical texts.

I believe Jesus is coming again in judgment.

> ²² Jesus said to His followers, "The time will come when you will wish you could see the Son of Man for one day. But you will not be able to. ²³ They will say to you, 'He is here,' or, 'He is there,' but do not follow them. ²⁴ When the Son of Man comes, He will be as lightning that shines from one part of the sky to the other." (Luke 17:22–24)

We read in Matthew 25:31–33,

> "³¹ When the Son of Man comes in his glory and all his angels are with him, he will sit on his glorious throne. ³² The people of every nation will be gathered in front of him. He will separate

them as a shepherd separates the sheep from the goats. ³³ He will put the sheep on his right but the goats on his left."

We are steeped in worldwide conflicts full of violence with particular focus on the savage attacks on Israel. Many colleges of America are revealing themselves to be poisonous pools of anti-Semitism that have misshaped the minds of own our children who shout slogans of genocide. The words they shout and the banners they carry are revolting to God. They shock us.

It is easy to feel defeated by the scale of global heresy that thrives on violence against Israel and everything Christian. The pain of seeing our own children joining this darkness that ends in death without Jesus seems more than we can stand.

We must draw comfort from Jesus Christ who saves us forever. Truly, the greatest conflict that never ceases is satan's manipulation of the world around us to defeat our faith within us. Lean into Jesus. Share Him with your children, your friends, and strangers so they may know Jesus. They may know the Truth. They may know His peace. Their sins may be washed away in His blood-shed grace.

⁶ Jesus saith unto him, I am the way, the truth, and the life: no man cometh unto the Father, but by me. (John 14:6)

Pray for those who may become goats on Jesus's left when He returns as our eternal King: "⁴¹ Then the king will say to those on his left, 'Get away from me! God has cursed you! Go into everlasting fire that was prepared for the devil and his angels!'" (Matthew 25:41).

Father, please grant us the courage to share Jesus at every opportunity.

Little Children

In Judaism, children come of age at thirteen years. In Orthodox communities, girls come of age at twelve and boys at thirteen. Mitzvahs ceremoniously mark the threshold into adulthood.

I believe this gives us some context for these words of Jesus:

> ^{13} Then people brought little children to Jesus for him to place his hands on them and pray for them. But the disciples rebuked them. ^{14} Jesus said, "Let the little children come to me, and do not hinder them, for the kingdom of heaven belongs to such as these." ^{15} When he had placed his hands on them, he went on from there. (Matthew 19:13–15)

Little children were younger ones guileless and trusting of adults, some may have been babes in arms. They may be cute distractions, but they were not to be taken seriously. Does that sound familiar?

It is our earliest human nature that is more closely aligned with what our heavenly Father wants for us. Young innocents, trusting, and quick to give our hearts without reservation. These noble traits fade away as we grow and experience the sinful nature of the adults we trust and love. They are not perfect after all. We cannot hide this from our children as they grow. Perhaps this experience gained during their interplay with Mom and Dad (if he is present today) begins to embarrass them as they look back on their childhood where they accepted us on blind faith, without doubt.

This closely follows the fall of mankind in the garden of Eden in that satan convinced Adam and Eve that God was not to be trusted or followed. In this single act, satan violated them twice. He convinced them falsely that God wasn't who He said He was. We know God is all that and more perfectly. And satan convinced them to act on his falsehood to break their holy relationship with their Creator.

Our heavenly Father is the "adult" we believed our parents to be. He is perfect, He is just. "^{16} For God so loved the world that he gave his one and only Son, that whoever believes in him shall not perish but have eternal life" (John 3:16). "^{16} And without controversy great is the mystery of godliness: God was manifest in the flesh, justified in the Spirit, seen of angels, preached unto the Gentiles, believed on in the world, received up into glory" (1 Timothy 3:16). Jesus Christ lived a perfectly innocent life, died with every one of our sins upon Himself on the cross, and rose from death after defeating satan, sin, and death in hell for us. He sits at the right hand of God, the Father waiting to return and judge us all. In faith, may we be little children again forever.

Prayer Works!

We believe that God hears our prayers and answers them. We may wish that He answered more closely in accordance with our wishes, but that discussion is not over prayer's effectiveness.

God's prophet, Jonah, prayed to our heavenly Father and heard His responses. God told Jonah to go to the city of Nineveh to call them down for their evil practices and announce that God was about to destroy them. Jonah refused out of fear of what would happen to him if he called these evil, violent people out and promised their destruction. This is the Jonah who was swallowed up by a large fish and delivered to the shore near Nineveh when God sank the boat Jonah was using to flee God's mission for him.

The story of Jonah illustrates that God does listen to prayer. He didn't answer Jonah's prayer as Jonah wished, but God clearly was listening and responding to Jonah. It also demonstrates that God may change His mind in response to prayer. When Jonah relented and delivered God's Word to Nineveh, the people listened.

> [4] Then Jonah began to go through the city one day's walk; and he cried out and said, "Yet forty days and Nineveh will be overthrown." [5] Then the people of Nineveh believed in God; and they called a fast and put on sackcloth from the greatest to the least of them. [6] When the word reached the king of Nineveh, he arose from his throne, laid aside his robe from him, covered himself with sackcloth and sat on the ashes. [7] He issued a proclamation and it said, "In Nineveh by the decree of the king and his nobles: Do not let man, beast, herd, or flock

> taste a thing. Do not let them eat or drink water. [8] But both man and beast must be covered with sackcloth; and let men call on God earnestly that each may turn from his wicked way and from the violence which is in his hands. [9] Who knows, God may turn and relent and withdraw His burning anger so that we will not perish." [10] When God saw their deeds, that they turned from their wicked way, then God relented concerning the calamity which He had declared He would bring upon them. And He did not do it. (Jonah 3:4–10)

Jonah was upset at this. God refused Jonah when he begged to be released from His mission for him. But God listened to these depraved sinners and changed His mind about destroying them when they prayed to Him. What's up with that!

God listens to everyone who prays, everyone! He answers every prayer in accordance with His will, not ours. On the night He was betrayed, Jesus prayed, "[42] Father, if you are willing, take this cup from me; yet not my will, but yours be done" (Luke 22:42). Thanks be to God! May we always follow Jesus's example. When in God we trust, we are saved forever.

What Matters Most?

In Paul's letter to the Corinthians describing how we should prepare for Christ's return, he lists a set of choices and desired circumstances that would make most of us very uneasy.

> [29] But this I say, brethren, the time has been shortened, so that from now on those who have wives should be as though they had none; [30] and those who weep, as though they did not weep; and those who rejoice, as though they did not rejoice; and those who buy, as though they did not possess; [31] and those who use the world, as

though they did not make full use of it; for the form of this world is passing away. (1 Corinthians 7:29–31)

Jesus's words regarding His return to us to establish His kingdom in judgment: "[36] But of that day and hour no one knows, not even the angels of heaven, but My Father only. [44] Therefore you also be ready, for the Son of Man is coming at an hour you do not expect" (Matthew 24:36, 44).

Paul's words provide us with a perspective most of us do not consider in depth. I pray for Christ's return to establish His kingdom on earth where sin will be no more. We can't know the details about Heaven.

We do not know that we are sinners all and that we will be sinners no longer in Heaven. We know, "[4] He will wipe away every tear from their eyes, and death shall be no more, neither shall there be mourning, nor crying, nor pain anymore, for the former things have passed away" (Revelation 21:4). We have no firsthand experience, but we read of Jesus being visited by Elijah and Moses on the mount,

[17] Six days later, Jesus took Peter, James, and John the brother of James and went up on a high mountain. They were all alone there. [2] While these followers watched him, Jesus was changed. His face became bright like the sun, and his clothes became white as light. [3] Then two men were there, talking with him. They were Moses and Elijah. (Matthew 17:1–3)

The saints who have gone home before us seem to remain themselves. Moses and Eligah had a conversation with Jesus. We cannot know all about Heaven.

Jesus tells us that Heaven has no place for tears, fears, or pain. "[14] Let not your heart be troubled: ye believe in God, believe also in me. [2] In my Father's house are many mansions: if it were not so, I would have told you. I go to prepare a place for you. [3] And if I go and prepare a place for you, I will come again, and receive you unto myself; that where I am, there ye may be also" (John 14:1–3).

It is faith that matters most. "In God we trust" are words to live by forever and ever. Amen.

Weakness of Love

We are constantly reminded of the "force of arms" which we deploy against one another as individuals and as nations. Human history is writ large with the conclusion that whoever wins the war writes history. Defense is undoubtedly one of the largest components of every advanced nation's budget. And of course, today's headlines feature more conflicts, death, and damage than we can hold in our minds. Some of the conflicts are thousands of years old. They may become quiet from time to time, but inevitably, they will flare again and again. Force is the application of human nature to settle difference, even if it means genocide.

This is obvious to anyone who reads history. Inevitably, it is equally obvious to anyone who studies violence as a tool for resolving conflict that it is futile. We need only ask ourselves if violence changes the beliefs of its victims. It doesn't and was never intended to do so. It is meant to convince those who disagree that they will suffer for expressing or pursuing their differences.

How terribly we have improved the method and delivery of violence against those who oppose us. We have gone from finding larger stones to throw to making weapons that can destroy our planet.

What is God's solution? It is free will. It is love. It is sacrifice. It is forgiveness for the open heart that accepts Jesus Christ and repents. We choose for ourselves between eternal life in Jesus Christ or death in satan.

> "[16] For God so loved the world, that He gave His only begotten Son, that whoever believes in Him shall not perish, but have eternal life." (John 3:16)

> ⁶ Jesus saith unto him, I am the way, the truth, and the life: no man cometh unto the Father, but by me. (John 14:6)

> ²⁴ Verily, verily, I say unto you, He that heareth my word, and believeth him that sent me, hath eternal life, and cometh not into judgment, but hath passed out of death into life. (John 5:24)

> ³⁶ Jesus answered, My kingdom is not of this world: if my kingdom were of this world, then would my servants fight, that I should not be delivered to the Jews: but now is my kingdom not from hence. (John 18:36)

> Before He was delivered into the hands that would murder Him, Jesus prayed, ⁴² Saying, Father, if thou be willing, remove this cup from me: nevertheless not my will, but thine, be done. (Luke 22:42)

What a courageous act of holy love.

God entered our flesh to extend an invitation for us to choose our eternal destination. He examines our hearts to admit into Heaven only those who return His love for them, in faith. Jesus chose to die for our sins in blessed weakness. "⁹ But he said to me, 'My grace is sufficient for you, for my power is made perfect in weakness'" (2 Corinthians 12:9). Choose God. Thanks be to God forever.

Welcome Home!

We read of the power of faith throughout the New Testament. Jesus tells of its power and declares that we are healed by our faith in Him. That seems confusing to me in that Jesus Christ the only begotten Son of God is the One filled with power granted to Him by His Father.

Here is one example:

> [27] The woman heard about Jesus, so she followed him with the other people and touched his coat. [28] She thought, "If I can just touch his clothes, that will be enough to heal me." [29] As soon as she touched his coat, her bleeding stopped. She felt that her body was healed from all the suffering. [30] Jesus immediately felt power go out from him, so he stopped and turned around. "Who touched my clothes?" he asked. [33] The woman knew that she was healed, so she came and bowed at Jesus's feet. She was shaking with fear. She told Jesus the whole story. [34] He said to her, "Dear woman, you are made well because you believed. Go in peace. You will not suffer anymore." (Mark 5:27–30, 33–34)

Another example is this, friends of a man with palsy tore open the roof of a house where Jesus was speaking and lowered their ill friend down to Him to be healed.

> [5] And Jesus seeing their faith saith unto the sick of the palsy, Son, thy sins are forgiven. [6] But there were certain of the scribes sitting there, and reasoning in their hearts, [7] Why doth this man thus speak? he blasphemeth: who can forgive sins but one, even God? [8] And straightway Jesus, perceiving in his spirit that they so reasoned within themselves, saith unto them, Why reason ye these things in your hearts? [9] Which is easier, to say to the sick of the palsy, Thy sins are forgiven; or to say, Arise, and take up thy bed, and walk? [10] But that ye may know that the Son of man hath authority on earth to forgive sins (he saith to the sick of the palsy), [11] I say unto thee, Arise, take up thy bed, and go unto thy house. [12] And he

arose, and straightway took up the bed, and went forth before them all; insomuch that they were all amazed, and glorified God, saying, We never saw it on this fashion. (Mark 2:5–12)

I believe Jesus is reminding us that we must have a loving relationship with Him. He has the power but only uses it for those who believe in Him and open ourselves to receive it. This loving relationship does so much more than heal us. God welcomes us back into His family when we love Him in faith. We come home where "⁴ He will wipe every tear from their eyes. There will be no more death' or mourning or crying or pain, for the old order of things has passed away" (Revelation 21:4). Thanks be to God!

His Word Eternal

Imagine if you will, men and women who live less than one hundred years predicting they will defeat the Word of God in Christ within their lifetimes. We are hearing this proudly proclaimed in America and around the world.

These are the same people who coordinate the systemic effort to erase our history and replace it with lies and distortions crafted to dismantle our republic. Ironically, they themselves are doomed to repeat history because they have ignored or distorted it.

Shortly before his own death, Vladimir Lenin said, "I expect to live long enough to attend the funeral of all religion" (see today's LCMS devotion). How many recall him? He was the founder of the Soviet Union. How many recall the Soviet Union?

History is storied with people and nations proclaimed "great" and "greatest" of all. Millions of books written across hundreds of years make these claims and are cited by individuals who come and go in decades. "²⁴ For all flesh is as grass, and all the glory of man as the flower of grass. The grass withereth, and the flower thereof falleth away" (1 Peter 1:24).

The Roman emperor, Caesar, declared war on Christianity. Under his rule, Christians were slaughtered for sport in the games of the Coliseum. Uncounted others were slain throughout the empire over many decades. Hitler determined to eradicate the Jews and supervised the most hideously efficient solution to the Jewish problem. His effort murdered more than nine million Jewish men, women, and children. The contemporary followers of Lenin are following his instructions to erase the history of those they wish to subdue or, better yet, rewrite it to teach them to hate their own country so they won't defend it. Many graduates and students at our Ivy League schools are convinced there was no extermination of Jews in Germany during WWII. They believe the Jews made it up for sympathy and power. These same people believe there is no God, especially a Christian God.

It is certain that much of our history is lost to time with or without efforts to hide it. It is more certain that the Holy Bible, the Word of God, will never be lost.

Jesus tells of His return.

> "31 When the Son of Man comes in his glory and all his angels are with him, he will sit on his glorious throne. 32 The people of every nation will be gathered in front of him. He will separate them as a shepherd separates the sheep from the goats. 33 He will put the sheep on his right but the goats on his left. (Matthew 25:31–33)

Christ will judge everyone according to His unchanging, eternal Word. Jesus said, "Heaven and earth shall pass away, but my words shall not pass away" (Matthew 24:35). Thanks be to God that those who know the Word of God in the Bible and the flesh of Jesus Christ will celebrate His return in His grace.

Fatally Shortsighted

As we live, we learn that we must plan ahead to succeed. As toddlers, we plan just one step at a time. Soon, we learn to plan much further ahead, a walk all the way across the room unassisted. Soon, we are graduating from high school, maybe going to college, and planning a career. Now, we are looking years ahead. Too soon, we are planning for the security of our children and retirement for our later years. How far we have come.

Some are recognized as outstanding achievers in every area of interest. A few bask in the credit from others for their accomplishments. Even fewer earn lifetime achievement awards. Rare individuals are raised up as examples to follow. We may be deeply impressed with them and seek to emulate them. They are all heroes in our flesh, with a few earning the GOAT (Greatest of All Time) title. I bet their mothers were so proud (dads too). And they accomplished all this in a single lifetime (eighty years or so).

According to our science, the earth is 4.5 billion years old, give or take. The nearest star (except the sun) is about 25 trillion miles away. Just last year, our scientists pegged the age of the universe at 13.8 billion years. Now the estimate is 26.7 billion years. How big is it? Present scientific wisdom says 93 billion light-years across. A single light-year is about 6 trillion miles (NASA). You do the math, it hurts my mortal head. According to many scientists, it all came into being in a single brilliant explosion of light and matter from nothing. That is called the big bang theory.

Let's compare that with God's perspective and accomplishments.

> [1] In the beginning God created the heavens and the earth. [3] And God said, "Let there be light," and there was light. [4] God saw that the light was good, and he separated the light from the darkness. [5] God called the light "day," and the darkness he called "night." And there was evening, and there was morning—the first day. (Genesis 1:1, 3–5)

The Holy Bible is God's Word for us. These verses were written at His direction many thousands of years before the big bang theory.

> [25] Jesus said to her, "I am the resurrection and the life. The one who believes in me will

live, even though they die; [26] and whoever lives by believing in me will never die. Do you believe this?" (John 11:25–26)

[6] Jesus saith unto him, I am the way, the truth, and the life: no man cometh unto the Father, but by me. (John 14:6)

[4] "He will wipe every tear from their eyes. There will be no more death or mourning or crying or pain, for the old order of things has passed away." (Revelation 21:4)

Let us lower our eyes to study His Word and lift our prayers to Him forever and ever. Amen. Take the long view, eternity.

Too Awesome

When God delivered the Jews from Egypt. God chose Moses as His prophet to deliver this commandment to the pharaoh, "Let my people go" (see Exodus 9). The pharaoh's refusal began an escalating series of demonstrations of our Lord's power directed against the pharaoh and the Egyptian people.

God instructed Moses every step of the way Moses trod on His behalf. Moses's announcements were not of his design. Moses revealed God's declarations to the world. It was God who separated the Red Sea to make a way for His people, Israel. It was God who drowned the Egyptians that were closing in on the fleeing Jews.

Once they were safely beyond the pharaoh's reach, God told Moses to gather His people to hear God Himself.

[6] And it came to pass on the third day, when it was morning, that there were thunders and lightnings, and a thick cloud upon the mount, and the voice of a trumpet exceeding loud; and all the people that were in the camp trembled. [17]

> And Moses brought forth the people out of the camp to meet God; and they stood at the nether part of the mount. ¹⁸ And Mount Sinai, the whole of it, smoked, because Jehovah descended upon it in fire; and the smoke thereof ascended as the smoke of a furnace, and the whole mount quaked greatly. ¹⁹ And when the voice of the trumpet waxed louder and louder, Moses spake, and God answered him by a voice. (Exodus 19:6, 17–19)

> ¹⁸ And all the people perceived the thunderings, and the lightnings, and the voice of the trumpet, and the mountain smoking: and when the people saw it, they trembled, and stood afar off. ¹⁹ And they said unto Moses, Speak thou with us, and we will hear; but let not God speak with us, lest we die. (Exodus 20:18–19)

Moses was God's prophet so they may hear His Word without fear. Before Moses died, he shared this with the Jews:

> ¹⁷ And Jehovah said unto me, "They have well said that which they have spoken. ¹⁸ I will raise them up a prophet from among their brethren, like unto thee; and I will put my words in his mouth, and he shall speak unto them all that I shall command him. ¹⁹ And it shall come to pass, that whosoever will not hearken unto my words which he shall speak in my name, I will require it of him." (Deuteronomy 18:17–19)

Thousands of years later at Jesus's baptism, "¹⁷ And a voice from heaven said, This is my Son, whom I love; with him I am well pleased" (Matthew 3:17).

Later, Peter, John, and James witnessed Christ's transfiguration and reported this, "³⁵ And then a voice came from the cloud, saying,

'This is My Son, My Chosen One; listen to Him!'" (Luke 9:35). Jesus is God speaking His Word in a fashion that doesn't frighten us. Jesus humbly delivers an awesome invitation to His eternal grace.

About the Author

Gary Hankins was born in Riverdale, Maryland, in 1948. He grew up in a family sometimes separated by circumstances beyond his mother's control. While his childhood may not be have been ideal, he credits the early presence of Jesus Christ in his life through the Holy Spirit with guiding him along paths he did not know he was following. Gary has often observed that as he looks back, he sees Him with him in his darkest and brightest moments. I least appreciated it.

Gary enlisted in the United States Air Force upon graduation from high school. He found himself in Nakhon Phanom, Thailand, along the Mekong River bordering Laos. This yearlong separation from his family became a time for introspection that further deepened his appreciation of Christ's presence in his life.

He became a police officer in Washington, DC, upon discharge from the USAF, where he served for twenty-two years before retiring and founding a small consulting firm for fourteen years before retiring again. Upon his return home, Gary joined a Lutheran church and focused on serving Jesus who has so richly blessed him throughout his life. Thanks be to God.

www.ingramcontent.com/pod-product-compliance
Lightning Source LLC
Chambersburg PA
CBHW030624310125
21142CB00042B/411